What People Are Saying

"The Thriving Hive is an enjoyable read about creating a people-centric culture that looks after the well-being of your team. There are lessons every leader and manager can take from this quick read on how to recognize and reward your people!"

Ann Rhoades, President – People Ink
Co-Founder and EVP, People – JetBlue Airways
VP, People – Southwest Airlines

"It's time for *Who Moved My Cheese* to step aside, as *The Thriving Hive* brings to light the next generation of leadership and organizational enhancement. Ryan effectively integrates well-doing into the well-being equation and provides an enjoyable ride for the reader along the way."

Brad Cooper, MSPT, MBA, ATC, CWCCEO
US Corporate Wellness Co-founder,
The Catalyst Coaching Institute

"Mari Ryan's *The Thriving Hive* is a fun and entertaining story that uses a beehive parable to convey the key ingredients that go into building a people-centric organization. It successfully illustrates why employee well-being isn't just a nice-to-have in today's workplace, but a business imperative."

David Shadovitz, Editor,
Human Resource Executive Magazine

The Thriving Hive

**How People-Centric Workplaces
Ignite Engagement and Fuel Results**

Mari Ryan, MBA, MHP

Jeanne
Thanks for all that
you do to create thriving
lives
Mari Ryan

Pequossette Press

The Thriving Hive: How People-Centric Workplaces
Ignite Engagement and Fuel Results
By Mari Ryan

Copyright © 2018 Mari Ryan

Pequossette Press
ISBN: 978-1-7324410-0-2

Beehive text illustrations by Rampel (Iwilldovector)

Contact:
Mari Ryan
info@pequossettepress.com

Printed in the United States of America

Even though the bee is small, there she is on the flower, doing something of value. And the value she creates there contributes to a larger ecosystem of value, in that mountain meadow, in that range of mountains, in the world and even the universe. And can't you just feel how happy she is?

– Jay Ebben
Painted Hives

Contents

In the Beginning

More meaningful than giving me a pay-check and benefits, this organization was looking after my well-being.

My first corporate job was as a clerk, coding premium payments at a life insurance company in Hartford, Connecticut. It wasn't a very intellectually challenging or stimulating job. But I learned pretty quickly that there was something really special about this workplace, and that the 1,800 other employees in the home office of this company and I were given something that was indeed exceptional.

When I wanted to have my teeth cleaned, I just made an appointment with the company's dental hygienist, and I never left the building. On my lunch hour I would go to the bowling alley in the home office basement, and there I participated in matches with people from all over the organization.

Being very early in my career, I didn't know what I wanted to do or even what my strengths were. I had the opportunity to join a Toastmasters group where I first learned about speaking. I had the opportunity for career testing that gave me guidance on understanding my strengths and skills. When I became proficient at my job and became bored, I spoke with my manager about what I could do to learn about the business. He suggested an industry education program and gave me time during my workday to study.

This was a mutual insurance company, owned by the policyholders. The leaders articulated the purpose of creating a beneficial investment for the policyholders. Everyone understood, that was our purpose, and we all worked toward that vision.

More meaningful than giving me a paycheck and benefits, this organization was looking after my well-being. Since it was my first job, I thought that all companies were like this. It wasn't until later in my career, having worked at all different kinds of organizations, of all sizes, that I came to appreciate how special this workplace was.

The leaders in this organization understood the essence of employee well-being and what that means from a business perspective as well as how that translates to business results. They understood the well-being imperative. Today more organizations are coming to this realization. They're seeing the connection between the well-being of their employees and the profitability of their business.

The idea for this book germinated for several years. I've always loved the parable format. Stories play such an important role in history and how we learn the lessons of life. Parables are often a characterization or an exaggeration of real life. You'll find that in some ways I've exaggerated the elements of life to create a vivid example. The comparisons may feel black and white as you are reading. We know that there is much more gray in real life.

In preparing to write this book, I interviewed ten CEOs. From their candid conversations I heard interesting stories about what it takes to create high-performing organizations, why culture is so important, and the necessity of taking care of your employees. I'm grateful to these individuals for their willingness to share with me their experience and wisdom. I've also drawn on my career experience of working in and consulting with organizations of all sizes, in many different industries. Some clients may recognize elements of their workplace in the story. I'm honored to learn from so many forward-thinking leaders in my career.

In writing this book, my goal is to help create a world in which all people are valued for who they are, and to create thriving people-centric workplaces that support and encourage the well-being of each person. This story shows why organizations should put their people first, and why the well-being of the workforce is the most valuable asset of any business that wants to succeed for the long-term.

Story Before the Story

Bees have six legs, five eyes and four wings.

Bob popped out of his chair when the doorbell rang. He was excited about his visit with Nancy. His energy belied a seventy-something's body in retirement. Bailey, the Cairn Terrier, jumped out of her dog bed and raced to the door to greet Nancy.

"Nancy, it is delightful to see you," Bob said while welcoming her with a wide grin. "How was the drive up?"

"It was a treat and so relaxing to have such a lovely day for the drive. It is beautiful here. I see why you consider this to be a special place," responded Nancy.

"Susan and I love living here full time. As you know, this was our weekend get-away home for decades. We couldn't have planned better. It is just the right size, with plenty of room for the grandkids to roam and romp.

"And who is this little pooch?" Nancy asked.

"This is Bailey, our head of security," joked Bob. "Come on in. How about a cup of tea?" Bob motioned for her to follow him.

"That's perfect," responded Nancy.

Bob and Nancy headed to the kitchen where Bob put the kettle on the stove and prepared the tea. As he did, Nancy said, "Bob, I'm so grateful that when I called, you suggested that I come up for a visit. It's been way too long since we've had any real time together. And there are some things that I want to talk with you about."

"We haven't had as many conversations recently as we did when I first retired, but I assumed you were handling things in your own way and that you didn't need as much of my help anymore," said Bob.

"Well, some of that is true. I've been trying to handle things my way, and," she paused then laughed, "you are a tough act to follow. I did want to do things my way and establish myself as the new CEO. And at the same time, I want to honor your legacy and the organization's history of success."

"You're the right person for the job – the natural person to step into my role, given your 10 years with the company, your great success as the leader of our sales organization during that time, and your natural leadership skills," said Bob.

"Thank you for your kind words, Bob."

Bob poured the hot water into the teapot and put it on a tray, along with cups and some freshly baked cake. "Let's sit over here by the window so you can see the garden. It is one of the things I love doing now that I'm retired."

"Wow, it looks like an English cottage garden. Bob, it's beautiful," exclaimed Nancy.

"Try some of this cake, it is my newest secret recipe. And the special ingredient is honey I'm harvesting from local beehives," said Bob.

"You certainly are keeping yourself busy," said Nancy helping herself to one of the honey cakes.

"It was an adjustment at first after I retired. We still only came up here on weekends. It took me a bit of time before I began to cut back on the nonprofit boards and other things that I had been doing. I am finding great fulfillment in some of my new hobbies."

As they sat at the table near the window and drank their tea, Bob sensed that Nancy was anxious. "Nancy, what's going on? You seem distracted."

"Nothing gets by you." She paused and looked into her teacup. "I am a little anxious. And have been for a while. Let me be honest. I'm struggling a bit with my role as CEO. There are a few signs that things aren't quite as good as they were when you handed the reins of the company to me. And the board of directors is asking for more and more detail about daily operations."

"Tell me what's going on. What are the symptoms?" said Bob.

"We're seeing an uptick in turnover. People don't seem quite as engaged as they used to be. For that matter they sometimes seem downright distracted and unfocused. And they most definitely don't seem to be energized. It's as if they've lost the sense of enthusiasm and excitement. We're still making our numbers, but something is not quite right, and I'm having trouble putting my finger on it. All this is going on while the industry dynamics are changing. We need both the people and the organization to be more agile to deal with the pace of change and the continual need to innovate."

"Any other signs?" asked Bob.

"We are working hard to attract a younger workforce, but the number of applications has dropped and the referrals from current employees aren't coming in the way they used to. You know how bringing in new people and training them in our way is one of our secrets for success and essential for our growth. Customer satisfaction also has taken a dip. It feels like some of the ways we've been doing things are no longer working."

"And you feel responsible," said Bob.

"Well yes, the buck stops with me," replied Nancy.

"Indeed it does," said Bob. "I think you are right that the way you've been doing things may no longer be as effective as it used to be. Once when the economy took a nosedive, I realized that what I had been doing wasn't going to work in the new reality."

"Thank you for that acknowledgement. It's good to know that you've had a similar experience," replied Nancy. "One more thing I'm worried about is that I feel like my own personal well-being is at risk. It feels like all I do is work. Now that my kids are in college, I'm able to focus on work in a way that I wasn't able to before. But that is taking a toll."

"I have to admit that this part surprises me. Given your background and discipline as an athlete, I would have assumed that you had this part nailed," said Bob.

"I know. Me too. But it is so easy to let life get in the way. Once that discipline begins to slip away, it is hard to get back to those healthy rituals that help with keeping balance in my life," replied Nancy. "I have to say, I really miss the flow feeling that I get when I'm running."

"When you called, you asked for my help. How can I be of most help to you?" asked Bob.

"It's such a relief to talk about what's going on. There aren't many places a CEO can vent. But I'm looking for advice. Now that you've been away from the day-to-day for a while and you know the backstory and how the company operates, what would be most helpful is to help me see some of my blind spots or those of the organization," replied Nancy sincerely. "I think I might be part of the problem. I recognize that so much of what I do sends messages to the people in the organization."

"We all have blind spots," Bob reflected. "Your strength is in your desire to excel and willingness to learn so you can do what is right both for yourself and the organization."

"I have an idea. Are you up for a walk?" asked Bob.

"Sure, it will be great to stretch my legs after the drive. Where to?" asked Nancy.

"I'd like to show you something I've discovered. It might provide some insights to the situations you just described. But first, we need some gear."

"Now I'm curious. What's this expedition we're going on?" Nancy asked jokingly. "But wait, let me finish my piece of cake. It is luscious!" She savored the last few bites, delicately smacking her lips to show Bob her appreciation.

"Bailey, you ready for a walk?" Bob asked as Bailey ran toward the door.

"Looks like you don't have to ask twice," laughed Nancy.

Bob and Nancy headed to the garden shed where Bob picked up a few items and handed them to Nancy. "You'll need to put these on if you're going to the hives with me," Bob instructed as he pointed to the white coveralls. While a bit too large and quite baggy, the overalls went on easily. Nancy was glad she had worn sensible shoes, which she wriggled through the pant legs. She slipped her arms through the sleeves and zipped up the front then took a moment to look around the shed.

"Wow, look at all the gear you have," commented Nancy. "You have quite a cottage industry going here." She observed neatly organized sections for each aspect of beekeeping. There was a section where Bob picked up the clothing he was offering her – coveralls, helmet with veil, and gloves. Another section displayed his hive tools and smokers. And yet another area was set up with equipment for honey extracting.

"You are right about that. I've been enthralled learning about bees. That's why I'm delighted to share with you what I'm observing and learning. Let me show you how this helmet and veil works. We don't have to put it on until we get to the hives." Bob proceeded to show Nancy the tips on how the netting fit over the helmet to protect from bee stings.

"Looks like we're headed on a safari," laughed Nancy.

"Not quite, just a walk through this meadow to where the beehives I've been tending are located. I think you'll find this as fascinating as I do," said Bob energetically.

Bob continued talking as they headed across the meadow. "I'm fortunate to live in a very special part of the country. It is noteworthy in that this is one of the only truly organic, sustainable agriculture areas in the United States."

"What exactly does that mean?" asked Nancy taking in the scenery.

"In essence it is a return to the way our ancestors farmed. The agricultural community has come together to plan how to grow their crops in a sustainable way without using pesticides of any kind. They take into consideration the interaction of the plants, the insects, and the needs of humans. To do this and to be able to fully support sustainability, they have adopted practices such as: planting native plants, planting crops in smaller acreages, as well as planting native habitats near the cropland. But it also goes beyond the way crops are planted and synthetic pesticides are reduced or eliminated. It is also about the way the businesses are managed, by looking after the safety and well-being of their workers, reducing energy consumption and greenhouse gases. All this works in harmony, so that there is a thriving ecosystem in which the bees can do their work of pollination and everyone benefits from the healthy food supply," said Bob.

"This is fascinating," said Nancy. "I guess I never appreciated how much goes into creating a truly healthy food supply."

As they continued their walk, Bob started to explain some aspects of bees to Nancy.

"As I'm sure you know, Nancy, honeybees do more than just produce honey and beeswax. They play a critical role in agriculture by pollinating fruits and vegetables, which form the most nutritious part of our diet. As I've been studying bees and observing the hives I'm tending, I've noticed that each hive is a community whose members are collaborating to achieve shared goals. They build smoothly functioning teams that are leveraging the power of democratic decision-making processes. I've also noticed that not every hive functions exactly the same way. Let me show you what I mean."

Dive Hive
Meet the Team

A bee's first orientation flight will last only five minutes.

The Dive Hive management team was seated at the table waiting for the queen to arrive. They always made sure they were in the room and ready to go before she arrived.

Benny, bespectacled and always with a pencil behind one antenna, is the Chief Financial Officer. He was ready to report the numbers, as he always does. Benny comes from a long line of bean counters. Both his father and grandfather were bean counters before him.

Sarge, a former military drill sergeant and the Chief of Operations, was ready to report on the field operations. Moving from the military to the private sector is an ongoing transition for Sarge. It took him a while to accept that all worker bees weren't going to fly in formation.

Kindra, the shy one and former bee teacher, was ready to report on the Workforce Operations (a beehive version of Human Resources). Kindra is a kind soul who is always looking for the best in everyone. She often finds it difficult to report bad news such as how many bees have died or to be the one to fire a worker bee.

The other team members arrived together. Dick, with a slick comb-back, is the Chief Sales Officer. Dick came from another much larger colony that had a reputation for producing large quantities of very low-quality honey. The rumor was they were diluting their honey by adding corn syrup.

And finally, Happy, a perpetually happy bee, is the Chief of Customer Satisfaction. Happy has the most positive attitude of any bee and may not seem like the ideal bee for this role, but happy customers are important, and she is good at keeping them happy.

A hush fell over the meeting comb as Queen Cruella entered. Whirring her wings and flouncing her barbed stinger, she moved to her position of power at the front of the boardroom table. The team members ducked slightly as they felt her piercing gaze steady on each of them one by one, then command all of their attention with her 300-degree all-encompassing vision. The meeting began.

"Give me the numbers," ordered Queen Cruella.

"I'll start with the good news," said Dick raising his head. "Our honey shipments are up by 20 percent this week. Our honey is in great demand. And I've been in touch with a new beauty care manufacturer that wants to base a whole line of products on our beeswax."

"I've got good news as well," said Happy. "Our customer returns and complaints are at an all-time low," she said proudly.

"Great news! Just what I wanted to hear," said Queen Cruella.

Dick and Happy were always a tough act to follow, especially when the other news wasn't good. "This week we are off our production goals by 10 percent. This is the second week in a row where production has dropped," reported Benny sheepishly, knowing she would be displeased with this report. He continued, "Our TPD [trips per day] numbers are decreasing as well, down to 90 from a high of 125 last month."

"How can that be? I thought you were going to get this problem fixed last week Sarge. What's going on?" she demanded.

"Well, I'm working on it, but we are continuing to see productivity drops. The bees aren't bringing back the amount of nectar we require for our production."

"What do our time per trip and load weight numbers look like?" asked Queen Cruella.

"Our trip time is 45 minutes per outing with an average weight of 30 milligrams of nectar. Both those numbers are also lower than they were last month," reported Benny.

"You all know that we can't be the largest producer of honey and beeswax in the county if we continue to miss our numbers. Keeping our production levels at peak or above is absolutely essential to achieve our target profit. Tell me what you've done so far and what are you doing to solve this problem?" stated Queen Cruella.

"In the past week, we gathered the colony to restate the foraging rules to ensure that everyone is trained properly," Sarge reported. "We met with the scouts to see how far they have been traveling and what they are finding in bloom. By expanding the foraging area from half a mile to one mile, we increased the available acreage from 2,000 acres to over 8,000 acres. We've created teams of pollen foragers and sent them to the areas the scouts identified in the expanded territory."

"Ranging further from the hive means fewer trips per day. You'll have to get everyone to fly faster. Tell me you have some other ways to increase productivity," demanded Queen Cruella.

"I'll get a training boot camp session going to build wing strength and capacity, so the foragers can fly further and faster," said Sarge.

"Clearly this is not enough. We need to do more to meet our profit numbers," complained Queen Cruella. "What do our headcount numbers look like?"

"We've got 50,000 bees in production today. In the brood, there are 5,000 each in the larva and pupa stages. They will come on line for production in two and three weeks respectively. We are closely monitoring the food supplies to the larva stage to ensure we are managing our costs," stated Kindra. "Your own egg production is continuing at a rate of 1,000 eggs per day, giving us another 5,000 larvae by the end of the week."

Kindra paused before she continued and looked down, not making eye contact with the queen. "And there is one more thing."

"What!?" shouted Queen Cruella, her barbed stinger twitching.

"There was a swarm that departed last week taking over 5,000 bees. The second swarm to depart in two weeks. Don't forget our daily death rate of 500 bees, which is also increasing."

"Damn. Those swarms couldn't have happened at a worse time. So what you're telling me is our workforce numbers are actually declining." Queen

Cruella was fuming. "We've got to turn this situation around right away!" she shouted.

"Well, we've come up with a few ideas of additional actions that might help us turn around these shortfalls and improve our numbers." Benny inserted.

"Speak up then. Let me hear your ideas," said Queen Cruella.

"To start with, we are thinking that if we could attach a small sensor to each forager, we would be able to collect highly accurate GPS data on their distances, speed traveled, and number of trips per day. I'd have a field day with all that data," Benny said gleefully. "A group of researchers from a startup came by to show us this new technology. They have shown us the software and tracking data that they get from the sensors. It is amazing and will give us highly accurate information that we never had before."

"I like that sensor idea. Having data on the movements of every worker bee is a great idea. But how much will that cost us? We can't miss our profit numbers," said Queen Cruella.

"This start-up has lots of venture capital funding but not a lot of clients or field experience to show the power of their sensors. They are practically giving it away," said Benny.

"Free is one of my favorite words," said Queen Cruella.

Sarge chimed in, "We've recently heard that some bee hummingbirds have been imported from Cuba to this area. We are hoping to enlist them as a contingent workforce and have them make nectar deposits nearby. Our carpenter bees are working on making a depository for them as we speak."

"What makes you think the bee hummingbirds will be willing to help by giving us their nectar?" asked Queen Cruella.

"Well, as recent immigrants, they are anxious to get settled in the area and find some work," said Sarge.

"Let me work up the numbers on how this is going to improve our daily nectar harvest, and I'll report back," said Benny.

"Let's see how things go this week. They better be heading in the right direction by next week," said Queen Cruella. With that, she quickly flitted away, without another word. As Queen Cruella departed, the team began their chant, "Long live the queen."

The following week, the team reassembled to give their weekly update on the numbers to Queen Cruella.

Dick skidded in just as the queen demanded, "Tell me there is good news this week."

Dick took the lead as usual. "Sales are still up. We're up another 10 percent this week. A new contract with a large chain of natural food stores was the big win for this week."

Happy rushed to report as well. "Customer satisfaction is still holding to our high standards."

Benny chimed in. "We were able to bring the bee hummingbirds from Cuba on line this week. Just as I surmised, they are willing to work for practically nothing to establish themselves. We are seeing increased nectar yields with their help. But overall our production numbers are still off. Our trips per day numbers are still below what we need; the quantity of nectar per bee is also slipping."

"We have 5,000 bees training in the forager boot camp to build strength for increasing their number of trips per day and trip distances," said Sarge. "I'm pushing them to the point of exhaustion. We restated the quotas on TPB and posted a leader board in hopes of stimulating some competition. We instituted new weighing procedures and trained the guard bees to inspect and measure the amount of pollen each forager is bringing back to the hive," reported Sarge. "We will discipline any bees that come back with a short haul."

Everyone could see the level of irritation growing as Queen Cruella listened to the reports.

"This is unacceptable. I told you three weeks ago that we needed to see our numbers improving and that's not happening. Here's what we are going to do," ordered the queen. "Call an all-wings meeting for five o'clock tomorrow morning. I'll make sure every bee in this colony understands why we are here, what is expected of him or her, and how we will hold everyone accountable. We'll raise the nectar quotas and increase working hours across all jobs types. No time off until we resolve this situation."

"Not even for family funerals?" Kindra winced.

"Not even for family funerals. And to keep them happy, we'll offer a bonus to each bee that overachieves the trips per day and daily weight numbers. Honey always talks!" said Queen Cruella.

"Yes ma'am," said Sarge. "I'll let everyone know."

"And one more thing. Kindra, I want you to begin working on the annual culling of the bottom 10 percent. Time to manage out those who can't carry their weight in nectar," ordered Queen Cruella.

As Queen Cruella departed, the team began their chant, "Long live the queen."

Dick and Happy flitted away before the rest of the team could ask them for any details on their reports. "I don't understand how he can be reporting improving sales when we are barely making our shipments to our existing customers. Where do you think all that honey is going?" asked Benny suspiciously.

"And, I'm not sure where all the returns are going. There was a huge return last week from the County General Store, one of our largest customers," said Kindra. "One of the bees told me before she left with the swarm."

"Something's not right here. Let's keep an eye on those two," said Sarge puffing out his broad chest. "I don't trust them as far as I can throw them."

Nancy and Bob
What Do You See?

Queens can live as long as two to three years.

"So what do you think?" asked Bob.

"This is fascinating, I had no clue how interesting and complex bees are," said Nancy.

"When I come out here and start working with the bees, the sensation is such a flow experience. I have no sense of time, place, or that anything exists except what I'm doing right in that moment," replied Bob.

"I can completely understand how that happens," said Nancy. "This is captivating."

"Well, I'm finding that interacting with the bees and observing how the hives operate inspires me to reflect on my business career," responded Bob.

"Say more," said Nancy.

"Well, when I look at this hive, it is functioning like we managed early in my career, and how we were taught in business school. It was all about the profit and the numbers. You can see the Queen's command and control approach. Haven't we all been that way at some point when the numbers are down?" replied Bob.

"I know what you mean," said Nancy. "I had the same experience in my career. Nothing mattered but the numbers, at the expense of everything else."

"Yes, and that's why I call this the Dive Hive. Now we both know that this isn't necessarily the right approach," considered Bob. "We know that the numbers are important in every business, but solely focusing on numbers is shortsighted."

"There are definitely downsides of managing this way," said Nancy. "I've lived through this myself." She paused, "And perhaps I still am at times. After all, profit is one of the key measures of success."

"Are there other things you noticed here?" asked Bob.

"Well, Queen Cruella's authoritarian leadership style, along with the singular focus on the numbers, is dated."

"I'm not sure she is doing much leading," commented Bob.

"You're right about that. It's hard to see how she can be building respect, trust, and a culture of collaboration with that style," added Nancy.

"There are definitely some interesting lessons we can learn here. Do you agree?" asked Bob.

"I never would have thought a beehive would be the place to show me these lessons in a way that helps me reflect on my own management style, but it absolutely is doing that," responded Nancy thoughtfully.

As Nancy reflects on what she's learning, she looks at Bob with an alarmed look on her face.

"Please tell me I'm not like Queen Cruella," said Nancy.

"No, you're not Queen Cruella," replied Bob with a chuckle. "Although when times are tough, there can be some Cruella in all of us."

"So I presume you would like to see more of the Dive Hive operations," Bob suggested.

Dive Hive
All-Wings Meeting

Bees sleep between five and eight hours a day, just like humans.

Night was slowly slipping away, as the pre-dawn light began to brighten the sky. The worker bees scurried as they gathered for the 5:00 a.m. Dive Hive all-wings meeting.

"Morning sure seems to come early," said Florence, a hard-working forager bee, as she rubbed the sleep out of her eyes.

"You got that right," said Samantha, a scout bee. "Feels like I am barely getting enough sleep to recharge my batteries."

Florence and Samantha are best friends, having grown up in the same brood. They've work closely together as foragers and scouts often do, and they also help other bees by supporting and encouraging them in their work.

"It will be interesting to see what happens at this morning's meeting. Sarge is relentless at how hard he has been working us these last few weeks," said Florence.

"I know. It is no surprise that so many bees are looking for a swarm to get them out of here," replied Samantha.

The colony came together precisely at 5:00 a.m. for the meeting. The senior leaders stood in back of the gathering near the rear of the hexagon where they could blend in with the other bees. A hush fell over the colony as Queen Cruella arrived.

"I've called you here today for a very important reason. I want to ensure that everyone fully understands our mission and what we are here to accomplish," said Queen Cruella in a commanding voice.

"As you know, my mother, her mother before her, and her mother before her established this hive with one purpose in mind: to make honey, lots and lots of honey. And why do we make honey? For profit. Without profit we won't be able to expand to make more honey to make more profit. We have established a territory that is unparalleled in this valley. From my earliest memories, my mother's warning has been instilled upon me. There are many, many other hives out there all willing to encroach and take our profits."

"Our goal is to be the largest producer of honey in the county. Nothing can interfere with our goal of producing more honey than any other hive, which in turn results in high profits. Is that clear?" demanded Queen Cruella.

A loud buzz arose from the worker bees, acknowledging the purpose of their work.

"Since you aren't making the numbers we need to achieve that goal, we are instituting some new policies," said Queen Cruella.

"First, effective immediately we are raising the nectar quotas for all foragers. Each bee that overachieves the trips per day and daily weight numbers will receive a bonus of 20 milligrams of additional honey per week during the foraging months," said Queen Cruella.

Florence and Samantha both cringed as the queen laid out the new policies. Getting more honey for fuel means the high performers will be able to fly further and gather more honey, but at the price of more time away from the hive and their families, more work. It would only have meaning if those bees took pride in their work.

"Additionally, we are increasing working hours across all jobs types. No time off under any circumstances until we resolve this situation. If the numbers don't improve in the next two weeks, we will begin round-the-clock shifts. We have no room for slackers here. Now get back to work," commanded Queen Cruella.

The bees chanted, "Long live the queen," as Queen Cruella exited the hexagon.

"I don't know how we are going to live up to her impossible demands," said Florence, who is usually perky and optimistic. "We're being asked to work longer hours, fly longer distances, fly faster, and carry more nectar. She is asking us to perform beyond anything we have ever dreamed possible."

"I know," acknowledged Samantha. "Everyone is so exhausted already. Most of the foragers aren't getting the amount of sleep they need to meet those kinds of numbers. I don't know how we are going to do this."

"If we try to keep up this pace, we're all going to die," whispered Florence.

"You got that right," said Samantha. "They have no idea what it is like for us. We never see the queen except for when she is dictating to us some new rule or policy. She lives up there in her ivory comb tower and has no clue about what our lives are like, or how hard we work."

As Florence and Samantha darted out of the hexagon, they could hear other bees grumbling about the new policies. They came across a cluster of bees. David, a drone bee; Sammy, a scout bee; Digger, an undertaker bee, and Hoover, a hygienic bee; were hovering nearby, looking very upset.

David commented to Florence and Samantha, "Sounds like you are as concerned as I am about all these productivity demands."

"We are indeed," responded Florence and Samantha simultaneously.

"The drones are truly unhappy; they have completely lost interest in the virgin queens. That's only going to complicate matters when the brood numbers start to decline and there are not enough new worker bees. Queen Cruella is only interested in one thing – profit."

"The scouts have to fly up to a mile away from the hive to find meadows with sufficient flowers. They are coming back too exhausted; they barely have the energy to do the waggle dance to tell the foragers where to find the flowers," said Sammy.

"We can't keep up with the volume of bees dying," said Digger.

"My team is so burned out that we can barely keep up with our task of keeping the hive clean," said Hoover.

As the group was comparing notes on their own and their colleagues' levels of exhaustion and burnout, Nettie, the queen's attending bee stopped by as Florence took off for another foraging flight.

"Nettie, I don't know how you do it," said Samantha. "It must be hard to work for Queen Cruella."

"You don't know the half of it," said Nettie. "She is too demanding. Always calling for more royal jelly. With all of the focus on gathering nectar for honey, I'm afraid that the pollen collection will fall and then what will we do. My babies will starve. My whole team of attendant bees is also exhausted and disheartened. It seems like no matter how hard we work, it is never enough."

"New shipments of nectar just arrived," announced Penelope, to the other bees in the pollen processing area.

"We need to keep this moving," said Pamela breathlessly. "Or you know what will happen."

"How is the output looking for this week?" asked Petunia. "Will we make the numbers?"

"How can I tell? No one tells me anything. All I do know is we can never make the numbers," screeched Penelope in a huff. "The production goals are totally unrealistic. They expect us to make more honey than any other hive."

"I know and look at the – pardon my French – crap honey we are turning out," said Piper. "We may produce the most, but everyone knows it is the worst tasting honey in the county."

"Next thing you know, they are going to be demanding that we create a whole new product line, maybe some of those stupid bee or flower shaped candies," said Petunia.

"That wouldn't surprise me," said Pamela in disgust.

"I heard that we are starting to produce royal jelly for export. It's a new fad and considered a super food," said Piper. "It is believed to extend life and slow aging."

"Well, it's certainly not slowing my aging," grumped Petunia. "It is more labor intensive than anything else we make."

"But you know Queen Cruella will love it, as it commands a very high price at the health food store," countered Penelope.

"Psst, Helen, are you there?" asked Harriet, the hygienic bee, as she peeked out of the comb she was cleaning.

"Yeah, I'm here. What's up?" replied Helen drearily from an adjacent comb.

"I'm bored to death with this job. How about you?" Harriet revealed readily.

"Same here," piped in Hazel rushing up with her broom in hand. "I just overhead you two talking. I thought I was the only one here bored to tears."

"Are you kidding, this job is the worst. All we do all day is clean up after other bees. How could there be anything the least bit interesting about this job?" asked Helen.

"I know, this is the only job I've ever had. I'll probably die cleaning out combs," said Hazel sadly. "It is such a dead-end job."

"What we do seems so pointless," added Harriet in agreement. "Maybe we should stop our cleaning one day to see if anyone even notices what we do."

"Now there's an idea," replied Helen with a scheming look on her face.

"Imagine what it must be like to be a forager bee, flying all over the place," pined Hazel. "I'd give up this job in a heartbeat for any other job in this hive."

6

Nancy and Bob
Yikes!

While the queen is responsible for leading a swarm, she has no decision-making role in the hive.

"Yikes, that's all a bit scary," exclaimed Nancy.

"What do you see going on in the Dive Hive?" asked Bob.

"Well, who would want to work there?" responded Nancy. "The tyrannical queen is going to kill her bees with the demands she is placing on them."

"And so it seems," replied Bob. "Imagine these are the workers in your organization. No wonder we see turnover, disengaged workers, and workplace injuries."

"No one should have to work in a place like the Dive Hive," said Nancy. "The culture seems like something from the early part of the Industrial Revolution. Not what we see today."

"And yet, we hear all the time about how disengaged employees are, how stressed and burned out they are, why turnover is high. It is happening today. Perhaps the influencing factors are different, but the end result is the same," said Bob. "I think we both accept there are times when we are very focused on productivity and the numbers as the goal. I also realize that businesses need to know their numbers, but they don't always tell you the whole story."

"Perhaps we need to be thinking about the unintended consequences and the real cost of that," replied Nancy. "What is the impact on the workers?"

"It makes me think about the values we espouse. What's most important? Is it the short-term results or the long-term growth?" pondered Bob.

"You're right in so many ways. These are all real issues today," replied Nancy. "It certainly gives me some things to think about in terms of the culture we are creating, how we treat our employees, and how we look after their well-being."

"Maybe a peek into another hive will give you some ideas about that. Let's look at what I like to call the Alive Hive," said Bob as he motioned for Nancy to follow along.

As they moved toward the second hive, Nancy pulled her mobile phone out of her pocket and glanced at it.

"No signal out here," stated Bob.

"Oh. Good thing, I'll enjoy being unplugged for a few hours. I think I look at this more out of habit than any real need to know what's going on," replied Nancy.

"I find it interesting how technology has taken us away from the present moment and the focus on our relationships," commented Bob.

"You are right. This could be one of my issues with being distracted," replied Nancy.

"Let's go see the next hive," said Bob, as he led the way.

Alive Hive
Meet Queen Leddy

Queenright is a term that means the queen is present and healthy.

Queen Leddy began her morning walkabout to see for herself how everything was going in the Alive Hive. Queen Leddy comes from a long line of queen bees that are known for their patient temperament and being good listeners. She learned a lot by watching her mother and grandmother as she was growing up.

Walking through the various work areas she heard a buzz everywhere in the colony. The energy and activity levels were palpable. She not only heard the buzz in the hive, but she felt the atmosphere in the brood, thinking how the temperature was perfect. The scent of the honey was dizzying.

Her first stop was the brood comb for her daily egg laying and to see how the future worker bees were developing. It was impossible for the queen to enter the nursery without notice, but her majesty conveyed confidence and reassurance that everything is okay. Queen Leddy hovered slowly, watching the busy bees closely. She noticed how focused each bee was on their tasks, whether it was feeding the brood, cleaning up the comb, or preparing the brood food.

She patiently hovered by the larvae that she laid weeks ago and counted the days until they would begin to hatch.

"Good morning, Queen Leddy," said Wilma the worker bee gleefully.

"Good morning Wilma," responded Queen Leddy. "How is everything going here today?"

"Fabulous. We've got a good healthy brood growing. We're just finishing up another morning mass feeding. They can't get enough of this worker jelly," Wilma said with a laugh.

"They are insatiable," quipped Queen Leddy nodding.

"And how are you today, Queen Leddy?" inquired Willow, another worker bee.

"Why, I'm marvelous! It is a beautiful, sunny day. I'm ready to do my work and then see how the rest of the hive is carrying on," replied Queen Leddy. The worker bees huddled around her as they started feeding and grooming her.

Willow breathed a sigh of relief before she spread the queenright message throughout the hive that the queen was happy, healthy, and laying eggs. The moment the queen begins to fail, the hive takes immediate action to rear her replacement. Since Queen Leddy is young and healthy, there is no concern right now.

Wilma and the other workers in the nursery looking after the larvae are truly busy bees, feeding them en masse constantly, as many as 800 times a day. Eventually, they will feed the larvae, as they grow older, individually as needed, 150 to 180 times per day.

"They sure do look happy and healthy," said Queen Leddy. "At this rate, you hardly need me."

"That'll never happen," said Wilma. "We would be out of business in no time without you. This group of nurse bees is learning so quickly. I think each new class is learning more quickly and jumping right in to do whatever work needs to be done."

"That's the way we like it," said Queen Leddy. "Now if you'll excuse me, I have a few thousand eggs to lay, so I can keep you and your team busy."

Off she went to begin her daily egg-laying duties. Queen Leddy moved majestically across the combs as she searched for empty combs. She moved quickly to deposit an egg in each cell, at the rate of one per minute. She deposits as many as 1,500 eggs each day. At the same time, she decides if the eggs will be fertilized (females) or unfertilized (males).

Queen Leddy finished up her daily egg laying and was about to head over to meet the newest group of worker bees ready to start work. But before that, she stopped by the Super Hexagon to see what was buzzing. The Super Hexagon is an enormous hexagon cell where bees come together to share ideas, to collaborate on projects, and to kick back and relax at the Honey Bar when they are on a work break. After all, bees are a face-to-face consensus seeking assembly. The Super Hexagon is the best place to see the members of the community working together to achieve their shared goals.

Hanging out at the Honey Bar is a great pastime for all bees, but especially the foragers. They mingle with the others until they become drowsy then head off for a good night's sleep. As busy as the bees are, they spend a lot of time sleeping and rest-ing. Sleep is critical to help maintain energy for all bees, regardless of their age or job.

It is also the place where the HON Board with its Hive Operations and Numbers monopolizes one side of the Hexagon, with its neon cells scrolling numbers. The HON Board shows the key performance indicators for the hive. All the key numbers that contribute to keeping the hive operational are visible for everyone to see. Complete transparency in these numbers, keeps all community members informed.

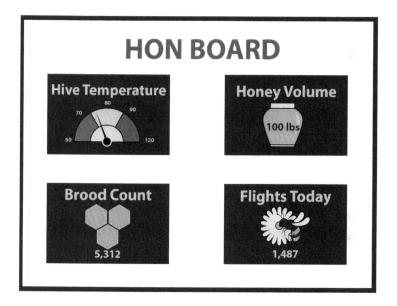

"Hey there Queen Leddy," said Chief Bee Scientist Stella. "Great to see you on this beautiful day."

"Yes, it is a lovely day. Nothing like a sunny spring day to perk up my wings," said Queen Leddy. "What are you working on?"

"I've been working with a small group of foragers who have identified what they think are some pesticides in the nectar they brought back," said Stella. "They found a new field of sunflowers that is bountiful, but they are concerned the nectar doesn't meet our quality standards. They want me to review their recommendations before telling the foragers not to go to this field."

"Please pass along my support to everyone. The power of the democratic decision making and the initiative they are taking to do what is right for the hive is commendable," said Queen Leddy. "Now, I'm off for a field trip with a new class of worker bees."

"Have a great time!" said Stella.

"Good morning Queen Leddy," said Tanya, the training and development team manager.

"Good morning, Tanya," said Queen Leddy. "Is your group ready to go?"

"They are ready and raring to go. They sure are eager to get started," said Tanya.

"Well then, let's get to it," said Queen Leddy.

It has been three weeks since these bees had grown from pupae to adults. They have all been working inside the hive doing general inside work, such as cleaning, feeding, building comb, ripening honey, and packing pollen. They are now ready to do tasks that involve flight. This is Queen Leddy's favorite daily task. She uses this opportunity to welcome them and send them off with a good start.

The buzz call could be heard, as Tanya wiggled her upper lip and whistled to bring the group to attention.

"Good morning team. It is my pleasure to introduce our revered but eminently approachable leader Queen Leddy," said Tanya.

A joyous buzz was heard as the new class of worker bees waited to be addressed by Queen Leddy. She stood among the worker bees, where they could see her up close and directly interact with her.

"Welcome, welcome, welcome. I'm glad to be here with you today," started Queen Leddy. "There is nothing more important in this hive than getting each new class of worker bees off to a great start. We do this with all of our worker bees and recognize it as a key part of the way things work in this colony. I want to tell you about our purpose for being here, our vision for how we can have impact in the world, and how together we can accomplish our goals."

"Each and every one of you has a significant role. It doesn't matter if you are inside bees, doing the work within the colony, or outside bees, doing work in the field, each and every job is equally as important," Queen Leddy continued. "It is our job to ensure that the people of this planet have healthy food to eat. We are responsible for pollinating over one third of the fruits, vegetables, berries, seeds, and nuts that make up a balanced diet.

Without us doing our work every day, there would be far fewer healthy people, farmers markets would cease to exist, and a vast variety of the produce in grocery stores would begin to disappear. Our purpose in life is to keep the planet and its people healthy. We have a vision of a world in which everyone eats fruits and vegetables as a part of every meal. They can't do that if we aren't doing our job."

A roar arose from the class of worker bees, who began to understand their part in this bigger purpose and to learn that the work they do every day makes a difference in ways they couldn't imagine.

As the roar died down, Queen Leddy went on, "Regardless of your individual job, whether you are tending the brood, cap cleaning, foraging for nectar, cleaning debris, packing pollen, comb building, ventilating, or guarding, each job is essential for our success and our survival. We work together as an integrated team to fulfill our purpose."

She continued, "We believe when you feel connected to this purpose, you will understand how the work you do every day contributes to something meaningful. We want you to feel passionate about your individual job, knowing that it is part of something bigger."

The worker bees were abuzz.

"To start you off on the right wing, we have a special first-day activity. We are all heading out for a field trip to a local farm and farmers market so you can personally see the impact of your work," said Queen Leddy, her eyes gleaming. "We start each class of worker bees this way, so that each day you can recall seeing the impact your work has in the world. This is also very special, since some of you will have inside jobs and may not otherwise have the opportunity to see for yourselves what your coworkers are doing."

"Before we head out, I want to give you a chance to ask questions or to share any thoughts you might have," said Queen Leddy.

"I'm so proud to be part of this colony," said Betty, a cheerful bouncing bee as she flew above the class. "Knowing that our work fulfills such an important purpose is exciting," she bubbled.

"Go ahead." Iris nudged her friend Ingrid. They had been best friends from the time they were larvae. "She won't sting you."

"I'm confused," Ingrid said sheepishly. Ingrid is a shy, introverted bee. "But what about the honey? I thought the reason we are here is to make honey."

"What a great question, Ingrid," said the queen. "I'm glad you had the courage to speak up. Honey is essential for our colony in several ways. First honey is our food and our fuel. Without it, we can't survive. The whole time you were in the brood, you were chowing down on the worker jelly provided by the nurse bees. And honey is also a by-product of our work. We have enough surplus honey that is sold at the farmers market we'll be visiting. And you should know, we make some of the best honey in the county. We're very proud of the quality honey we produce. It sweetens up the world when used in all sorts of products, such as baked goods.

Beeswax plays a contributing role in our colony as well. We use it for our comb cells for honey-storage, and larval and pupal protection within the hive. But there is always excess beeswax, which others use in making cosmetics and candles."

"Any other questions before we head out?" asked Queen Leddy. Hearing none, she continued, "I'll be joining you, along with our head scout bee Sybil. So, let's have at it women! Let's go keep this planet healthy."

"Follow me, we're off for a great day of flying and seeing where and how our work helps in the world outside the hive," said Head Scout Sybil.

Sybil led the way as the class of worker bees headed out on their field trip. Sybil loves these excursions as much as Queen Leddy. As head scout she's found the perfect farm that practices sustainable farming, so she can show the new worker bees some of the very important aspects of how the ecosystem works together to create healthier plant life.

"We are good. The pollen count is at 80 percent," said Paula, a pollen production bee.

"But how does it taste?" asked Petal, Paula's teammate in production, as she and other production team bees anxiously waited for the taste test results.

"It is fabulous. It's not just the flavor, it's also the texture that is sublime," replied Paula. "I think this is some of the best wildflower honey we've ever produced. I can't wait until Primrose tries this."

"I'm amazed at how our scouts and foragers are able to find early spring wildflowers blooming," said Paisley.

"Did I hear my name?" asked Primrose, the head of production, as she came into the pollen production area.

"I'm eager for you to try this wildflower honey. I think this is possibly our best ever," exclaimed Paula.

"I'd love a sample," said Primrose, as she took a small sample of the honey from Paula. "Wow, you are right. This is special. I love the texture. Whatever you are doing team, keep up the good work!"

"I'll get that quality score shining on the HON Board in the Super Hexagon so everyone knows we've got a great batch in the works," replied Petal.

"This is going to sell out in no time at the farmers market," said Primrose.

"And that county fair is coming up soon. Maybe we'll win a blue ribbon in the artisanal category," rejoined Petal.

8

Nancy and Bob
What a Difference!

In honeybee colonies, the old queen leads the swarm with a new queen staying behind.

"Tell me what you are seeing here," responded Bob.

"Wow, what a difference!" exclaimed Nancy. "I see why you call this the Alive Hive."

"There is such a different vibe here," said Bob laughing. "Pun intended."

"Absolutely," replied Nancy. "You nailed it. The vibe is completely different. It is much more relaxed, yet still highly productive."

Nancy continued, "I'm getting the sense that every bee is working toward a purpose that is far bigger than each of them individually. And they know how their work contributes to that purpose."

"Exactly, it's not all about the numbers or the profit," said Bob. "It's about something that has a much bigger impact, and of greater value, the meaning."

"What's also noticeable is that every worker is not only connected to that meaning, but they also feel valued for the contribution they are making to the purpose," added Nancy.

"At the very basic level, our job as leaders is to create an environment where each person and their contributions are valued," said Bob. "When we do that, so many other things fall into place."

"You know, I've thought about this a lot lately. On both a professional and personal level," replied Nancy. "The whole concept of purpose, vision, and mission are fundamental to leading a meaningful life and doing meaningful work, and how we help the employees make that connection."

"I wish I had the same revelations that you are having now, much earlier in my life and my career," said Bob in a contemplative tone of voice. "I would have spent far less time beating myself up and focusing on the wrong things."

"I'm with you on that," said Nancy. "Look at how excited the bees are to be part of this and how engaged they are."

"They are on board with the purpose they are here to fulfill," commented Bob. "What this speaks to is intrinsic motivation. Until you tap into both your own and the employees' intrinsic motivation, you aren't running on all cylinders."

"What is also apparent is a completely different leadership style. Here it is respectful, supportive, and encouraging. Queen Leddy's walking around and being visible, as opposed to the command and control approach, is a huge difference," said Nancy.

"Did you notice how everyone seems to feel genuinely cared for and valued?" asked Bob.

"That is so evident," replied Nancy.

"And what about the numbers?" asked Bob. "Who's minding the numbers?"

"Well, it looks like everyone is. There is such transparency," commented Nancy. "Now that's a different approach."

"So you can see how different these hives are," said Bob.

"That goes without saying," replied Nancy.

"Enough for one day?" asked Bob.

"I'm so captivated, I'm not sure I want to leave," said Nancy.

"You see, that's exactly how I feel when I'm out here," agreed Bob. "Let's see what happens next. Bailey, let's go."

Alive Hive
Busy Bees at Work

Foragers perform a dance called the waggle dance to communicate the distance and direction to pollen sources.

"Welcome back squad," said Gertrude, the imposing guard bee to the returning foragers. Gertrude, an older bee, is well known as the protector of the hive. She patrols the hive opening, checks every single bee coming in, and prevents unwanted intruders from entering. Her menacing demeanor intimidates new foragers when they first meet her. But once they realize how welcoming she is to members of her colony, they respect how scary she looks in her role as a guard bee.

"Nice to be back and look at this haul," gushed Filia, an experienced forager. "You wouldn't believe the fields of flowering plants and trees in bloom where we are harvesting nectar. The flowers are beautiful and bountiful. Our scouts are the best ever in finding this amazing place for us to collect and pollinate."

"It is pretty amazing that you are finding so much in bloom, given that it's been so dry," inserted Gina, Gertrude's capable assistant guard bee.

"You are right. Our scouts sure gave us a gift when they found this meadow. It's near a small brook and there is still enough moisture for plants to flower," said Fleta breathlessly, the forager best known for her swift flying. "I hit a personal record on that trip with 100 flower visits."

"Congratulations Fleta. Great work. You know, we've got quite a crew here," said Gertrude proudly.

Filia, Fleta, and the other returning foragers headed to the unloading zone where they were met by Holly and a group of other house bees.

"We heard about your great bounty," said Holly in a congratulatory tone.

"Word travels fast," said Filia with a chuckle. "There are no secrets in this hive."

Each forager dropped their pollen loads to two or three house bees. From there the house bees moved off to a quiet area where they will process the nectar to prevent fermentation.

"You've got some great looking pollen here," said Heather, another industrious house bee. "Filia, it looks like you pulled in a great load of maple pollen. Look at how colorful it is."

"Yes, the maples are beginning to bloom. You sure know your pollen, Heather," replied Filia.

"I'll bet you're ready for some rest now," said Holly.

"You've got that right," said Fleta. "I'm looking forward to some quality down time especially after a record-setting day."

"How long before the bee bread will be ready?" asked Filia.

"Give us about 30 minutes," said Holly. "We'll bring it to the lounge area in the Super Hexagon. You take it easy. We've got the pollen processing under control."

"Do you see them yet," Eman, an engineering bee, anxiously asked Gertrude.

"Not yet, but I'm confident they will be here soon," responded Gertrude.

"Our hive temperature is rising, we need that water delivery *now*," roared Eman.

"Eman, please maintain your composure. You can trust our bee sisters in the water brigade to do their job," said Gertrude patiently as she returned to her guard post viewing the green landscape surrounding the hive entrance.

"Eyes up everyone," shouted Gertrude. "We've got a water brigade returning. They get first priority to unload."

The bees in the unloading area, scuffled off to the side to make room for the water brigade's delivery. They always get first unloading priority, since maintaining hive temperature is critical.

Filia, Fleta, and the foragers headed to the Super Hexagon to prep for tomorrow's foraging and to begin their well-deserved rest. They would now have an extended period of relaxing and eating the nourishing bee bread. They need lots of sleep to recharge their energy before the next day's foraging flights.

"I'm starving," said Fleta as she pulled into the café and eyed the honey pot on the counter. "The quality of the honey keeps getting better and better."

The bees were buzzing about in the Super Hexagon, catching up on the latest news, hanging out, and playing bee games (such as Ring Around the Posey and Kick Pollen). The whole colony comes together in the Super Hexagon for social time, mingling with their colleagues to learn about new projects going on within the hive, and to have fun. The Super Hexagon is the hub of the hive, helping keep information flowing and relationships thriving.

"Great news," said Scout Sabra excitedly. "I've found an enormous field of flowers in bloom. Let me give you the specs for tomorrow's flights."

Filia, Fleta, and the other foragers circled around Sabra and paid close attention.

"Oh my, I'm too excited to talk about it." With that introduction, Sabra launched into a waggle dance, rubbing her wings together, causing vibrations on the comb. Her dance consisted of flying in circles and figure eights. She shared the location of the next day's food source, highlighting landmarks, the distance to the flowers, and the location of a nearby water supply.

"Thanks Sabra, great info. I know we'll have no trouble finding it," said Fleta. "I'll sleep well tonight thinking about that field of flowers."

"Wendy, did you get that info on the water source?" asked Filia.

"You bet. Got it," said Wendy, a water forager.

Suddenly, a cheer could be heard throughout the Super Hexagon.

"What's that?" asked Sabra curiously.

"Looks like our honey volume from this morning's foraging were just posted to the HON Board. Everyone is excited about the big haul," said Filia. "And we have you to thank. That was a great source you found for today's forage."

"How great it feels that we get all this information so quickly and everyone knows exactly what is going on throughout the hive," responded Sabra. "I'll sleep well tonight, too, knowing that everything is on track."

Back at the pollen processing area, the house bees were busy curing the pollen into bee bread.

"Hedda, it looks like you're struggling. Do you need any help there?" asked Holly.

"Did you read my mind? I was just thinking that I could use a few more assistants. This sure is a big load," responded Hedda gratefully. "Thanks so much for noticing and being there to support me."

"Let me round up a few more house bees to help us out. We'll get this load processed in no time," said Holly.

Adjacent to the pollen processing area, the house bees were busy packing the pollen into cells. After they finish, they put a small coat of honey over the outside of the cell to act as a preserver.

Nancy and Bob Collaboration

While a worker bee can chew its way out of the birthing cell, drones need other bees to help.

"How does this look and feel to you?" asked Bob.

"This is equally fascinating, on so many different levels," said Nancy. "To start with, this organization is very flat. It seems the workers are empowered. They are collaborative and collegial. The teamwork is amazing."

"It does feel very different," said Bob.

"None of the bees seem overly stressed. They are fully engaged, focusing on their individual jobs," replied Nancy.

"Notice anything else?" asked Bob.

"The feeling here is very different. It appears there is strong trust in the worker bees to do their job and to make decisions. The culture is completely different," said Nancy.

"Culture sets the tone for the whole operation," said Bob. "I wish I had paid more attention to culture when I was a leader. Sometimes the culture took on a life of its own, based on our shared experiences. It wasn't something we deliberately thought about or guided."

"You are right. There are so many aspects of culture that I take for granted. I have to constantly remind myself that the leaders of the organization define the culture through their actions, as well as their words," said Nancy.

"Exactly," said Bob with an affirming nod of his head.

"This certainly gives me a new way of looking at our culture and how the employees are feeling about their workplace," said Nancy pensively.

"Had enough for one day?" asked Bob.

"I can't tell you how much this gives me to think about in terms of our own organization, leadership style, and the way we care for employees," said Nancy.

"I knew you'd feel that way," said Bob.

"Can I come back to observe and learn another time?" asked Nancy.

"Consider it an open invitation," replied Bob with a smile.

Bob looked up from his book as he heard the phone ring. He leaned toward the side table next to his reading chair to pick up the handset, noticing from the caller id that Nancy was calling.

"Well hello," said Bob jovially.

"Hi there, did I catch you at a good time?" asked Nancy.

"Absolutely. It is raining today, so I'm catching up on some reading," responded Bob.

"I had such as great time getting together with you and especially with the visit to your hives," started Nancy. "And I will confess, the honey cake never made it home. I snacked along the way on the drive back."

"I'm delighted that you had a good time and that you enjoyed the honey cake," said Bob with a chuckle. "That honey cake has been a big hit."

"I want to tell you about some things I've been thinking about since my visit. I was struck by what I saw in the hives. It has given me a lot to think about regarding the company and some of the issues that we talked about," said Nancy.

"Well, I have to say I'm delighted that you are giving this so much thought," replied Bob.

"Actually, I'm doing more than just thinking about it. I'm doing some things differently as a result," said Nancy. "To start with, I'm spending more time walking around. I don't learn much sitting in my office. And I'm focused on listening. Really listening to what my colleagues and employees are saying. What they are concerned about."

"And what are you hearing?" asked Bob.

"I'm hearing that there may be better ways to do things than what we are doing now. And that many of the employees don't feel empowered to move forward with their ideas. I think we need to begin looking at different ways to organize and empower our teams," replied Nancy.

"That's big," acknowledged Bob.

"I know. And it feels good to be thinking about these kinds of changes and starting to move forward with them," said Nancy.

"I'll bet the employees will feel the same way," agreed Bob.

"I've also asked my colleagues to try an experiment. In our meetings, we're creating technology free zones, meaning no cell phones or computers, except as needed for the specific work," said Nancy.

"I'll bet that made a few people uncomfortable," replied Bob.

"Well, it is interesting. While a few people resisted at first, they soon realized how much more focused and productive we all are. Our meetings finish sooner, and everyone feels more connected," added Nancy.

"Isn't it interesting how a small change can have such impact," said Bob.

"One more thing I'm doing," Nancy continued. "I invited everyone in the company to join me on the Cross-County Trek fundraising bike ride – either as a rider or a volunteer. You recall how much I used to cycle. I even offered to buy bikes and helmets for anyone who didn't have them. It feels good to be exercising regularly again."

"What fun. How many people signed up?" asked Bob

"I was amazed at the response. We have a group of 30 riders and over 50 volunteers, including most of my leadership team. It's going to be a blast. Want to join us?" asked Nancy.

"Now that's a challenge I will definitely consider," replied Bob with a chuckle.

"I'm wondering if I could come up for another visit?" asked Nancy.

"Absolutely, you know you are welcome here anytime," replied Bob with a wide grin. "Bring your bike."

Reflection Questions

Take a few minutes to reflect as Nancy did on how your organization resembles the Dive Hive and the Alive Hive. Use these questions as a guide in your reflection.

Your Organization

- How does the culture of your organization connect the people to its purpose, mission, and vision?
- What are the values that your organization espouses? To what extent is respect for all people at the core of those values?

- How does the culture care for people first in your organization? How is that demonstrated?

- How does investing in a culture focused on people translate to bottom-line impact?

Managing Oneself

- How are your personal values aligned with those of the organization?

- How connected do you feel to the purpose and mission of the organization?

- What are your personal habits and rituals that help you be your best every day?

- How can you be a role model for others in putting people first? If not to a great extent, what can you do differently or in addition to what you are doing now?

Dive Hive
Overheating!

Bees' wings flap 12,000 to 15,000 times per minute just to keep their pollen-laden bodies aloft.

"Incoming!" bellowed Goldie, the younger of the guard bees on duty at the Dive Hive.

"Oh no!" shouted Gjerta, the protective guard bee, as she faced the hive opening.

Grizelda, the gray-haired shift supervisor turned toward the hive opening just in time to see why Gjerta was upset. Half a dozen bees were a short distance from the hive entrance when they fell to the ground.

"Oh boy, this looks like it isn't an isolated situation," said Grizelda.

As they all looked toward the hive opening, they could see that about a fifth of the bees that were returning from foraging were falling short of the hive entrance. The fall to the ground from the height of the hive was almost always fatal.

At that moment, Gjerta raced to the edge of the hive to grab several gasping foragers just before they plunged over the edge.

"I'm so grateful you were here to help," said Filia the first of the foragers. "I was completely stressed all the way back."

"We had to go so far, and with the extra nectar load demanded by Queen Cruella, we were over-weight," panted Flora. "I thought I was doomed."

"Have you seen the water bees?" asked Gjerta.

"We saw them on the way out. But the wetlands are drying up, so they had to go in search of a new water source," said Filia. "I hope they make it back."

"What's happening?" asked Goldie, having never seen this type of catastrophe before.

"They are out of fuel," said Gjerta hesitantly. "If they carry too much nectar and at the same time don't have enough honey for fuel, they can't keep up their strength and they crash."

"Don't let word of this get to Benny, or we'll never hear the end of it," said Grizelda.

"Is there anything we can do to help them?" asked Goldie.

"I'm afraid not," responded Gjerta. "When they miscalculate load and fueling requirements, unfortunately, it is all over for them. So much is involved in these calculations. The scouts tell them where to find the nectar or water. If it is windy, or if they exceed the distances set or try to carry more weight in pollen and nectar, well, the results aren't good. It looks like most are making it back safely. But they are far more exhausted than usual. It looks like they are exceeding the nectar and pollen limits set for a safe return."

"Will the water foragers have the same problem?" naively asked Goldie.

"Let's hope not," said Gjerta, "We are on critical standby for the water supply."

"We need water now!" shouted Wilma, the worker bee supervising the Brood Temperature Department. "Where is it?"

"No sign of them yet," responded Wanda, looking toward the landing area for the returning water foraging bees. "If we don't get some relief in here soon, this brood will be cooked."

"We can't wait any longer, it's getting too hot. Recruit more worker bees to get in here and start fanning the brood comb," demanded Wilma.

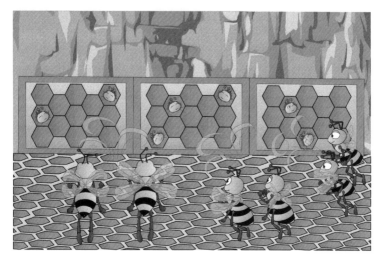

"I'll get another group to start heat shielding," said Wanda, as she directed a group of worker bees to press their bodies against the brood nest wall to absorb the excess heat.

Wilma closely monitored the situation for the next ten minutes by keeping an eye on the brood thermometers. When she saw that the temperatures were returning to a safe level, she gave the command: "Shielding cease!"

"Let's hope this drought ends soon," responded Wanda. "It is the worst in anyone's memory."

"It is definitely taking a toll on us," said Wilma sadly.

Sarge walked into the drone lounge where he noticed half a dozen drones lying around, doing nothing.

"Why are you hanging out doing nothing?" Sarge demanded. His face was bright red, and he looked overheated. "Why aren't you working?"

"We're done for today," replied Danny, the larger of the drones, in an off the wing manner. "Our work is finished."

"But... but...," Sarge stumbled over his words, before starting to swoon.

"Sarge, you okay?" asked Danny.

Sarge grabbed at this chest and gasped for breath as he tumbled over. It looked like he was unconscious.

"Danny, quick, do something!" exclaimed Doran, as he jumped off the lounge chair and raced to Sarge's side. "What do you think has happened?"

"I'm not sure. His face was sure red, and he was all upset when he flew in. "Maybe he's had a heart attack," replied Danny.

"Well, we all know he's not the healthiest specimen. With being overweight and all the cigars he smokes," commented Doran. "And you know how super stressed everyone is."

"The end is near, the end is near," wailed Nelly, the nervous nurse bee.

"The brood is doomed and we're all going to die," countered Nitzie another nurse bee.

"Overheating, water shortage, heat wave, what a catastrophe! And Queen Cruella demanding more and more," exclaimed Natalie.

"By the way, has anyone seen Queen Cruella? Where are the leaders when we need them most?" asked Nitzie.

"What's going to happen to us?" asked Wava, a young worker bee huddled with several other young bees.

"Is this the end of us and our hive?" asked Whim. "I heard from another comb that they were grabbing all the honey they could get and hunkering down to see if they can survive."

The brood nurse and worker bees are overcome with fear and panic as they hear of the issues that the colony is currently experiencing. They huddle together and buzz about all the terrible things that are happening to the hive, as they await a member of the leadership team to tell them what to do next.

"We've got to get out of here," Whitney, a strong-willed worker bee, asserted.

"Who is with us? We need to get a swarm moving before this hive collapses around us," encouraged Winter to the group of bees huddled in the comb.

"If we don't swarm soon, we'll all be dead," proclaimed Willa fearfully and with panic in her voice.

"How many bees do you think we can round up?" asked Whitney, as she began to plot their departure.

"Let's find a few scout bees. How much time do you think they need to scout out a new hive location?" asked Wilma.

"That will take hours, perhaps all day," said Winter. "And then they are going to want to do that silly dance, to convince us that one location is better than another. I'm not sure we have that much time."

"How are the numbers looking?" asked Kindra of Benny, as she stepped into the cash comb.

"I'm sure having to sharpen my pencil to make sense of these," responded Benny scratching behind his antennae.

"How so?" asked Kindra curiously.

"Well, everything doesn't seem to add up. Dick keeps saying the sales look great and Happy keeps saying that the customers are all happy, yet we've had more returns than ever before," responded Benny as he continued to pour over the numbers. "I'm struggling to make the numbers work."

"What do we know about the returns?" asked Kindra.

"Well, not much. That's part of the problem," replied Benny.

"Benny, I stopped by because I want to talk with you about something that is concerning me. Do you have a moment?" asked Kindra.

Benny put his pencil behind his antenna and turned to face Kindra.

"What's up?" he asked.

"I've come to you because you seem to have more insights into what's going on than most of us on the leadership team. In all my years with Workforce Operations, I've never encountered a more dysfunctional workplace. I'm concerned about the welfare of our colony. There seems to be chaos everywhere I turn," replied Kindra feeling more bravado than ever before.

"There are so many things happening at once with the water shortage, foraging failures, overheating, and discontented bees everywhere. There is such poor communication. The bees aren't working together to solve problems. There's no collaboration.

"The well-being of every bee in the hive seems to be compromised in some way. But of most concern is that we seem to have no leadership helping us solve these problems. I sense we are on the verge of a mass swarm that will threaten the viability of the colony."

"Wow, I can see your concerns," said Benny half-focused.

"Have you heard about the number not making it back with their haul?" asked Kindra.

"No, this is the first I've heard about it," replied Benny as he turned back to his books. "I'm confident that if anyone can figure out these problems, it's you."

Kindra looked on in stunned silence as Benny returned to his numbers.

Nancy and Bob
More Observations

The cells used to create queens are different, peanut shaped, and much larger than other cells.

"So glad you arrived early," said Bob as he opened Nancy's car door in the driveway.

"It's another beautiful day. I appreciated the early start," replied Nancy as she handed Bob a box of macaroons from a shop near her house.

"You remembered, my favorites. You shouldn't have," replied Bob. "But I'm glad you did. How about some tea to go with these before we head out to the hives?"

"Perfect," said Nancy.

Half an hour later, Nancy and Bob ventured out to the hives after donning their protective gear. Bailey trailed closely behind. They stood by and observed the hive activity for a while before Bob nudged Nancy with his elbow.

"What do you think?" asked Bob.

"This is actually frightening," said Nancy in response to what she was seeing in the Dive Hive.

"Tell me what you're feeling in seeing this," encouraged Bob.

"Let's look at it first from the worker bee perspective. I'm feeling empathy for the worker bees. They are panicking, in fear for their well-being, their lives even. Also, they are getting no guidance or direction from their leaders. They feel alone and abandoned," replied Nancy.

"There are many lessons here," started Bob. "Clearly this hive is not ready for the threats that they are experiencing. There is little resilience here."

"And the leaders seem clueless!" exclaimed Nancy with a grimace.

"I agree," laughed Bob seeing Nancy's frustration. "Although it's not a laughing matter, since the viability of the hive is threatened by their lack of resilience and preparedness to handle adversity."

"It seems the leaders are so narrowly focused on their numbers and their own needs, that they are oblivious to the needs of their workers," said Nancy.

"Astute observation," acknowledged Bob.

"I also noticed that due to the leadership style, the workers are not empowered to solve problems. They are waiting for the leaders to solve them. It is only out of desperation and survival that the workers begin to take action," observed Nancy.

Nancy continued, "Fundamentally, the bees aren't aligned with profit as the purpose that the queen is driving. Additionally, there are communication problems resulting in the bees not working together or knowing what is going on."

"They are kept in the proverbial dark," agreed Bob.

"With all the things that are impacting the hive, it makes me think about all the external factors that influence our business. I wonder are we prepared to deal with them. Especially if several of them hit us at the same time, as is happening here," conceded Nancy.

Alive Hive
Pulling Together

Bees collect pollen, nectar, and water.

"I've called you all together today to ask for your help," said Queen Leddy standing in the center of the Super Hexagon of the Alive Hive.

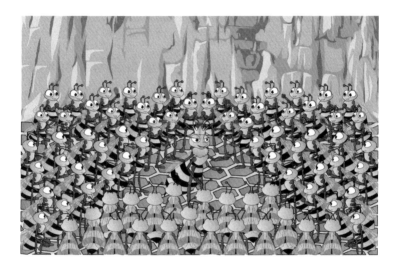

"What I'm about to say is not news; you all know what is going on. A perfect storm is brewing. The drought continues making water nearly impossible to find, the high outdoor temperatures continue unabated, both of which are threatening the brood. And we have an overcrowding situation, which is contributing to the internal heat problem. You have always done a great job working in teams coming up with solutions. Now is your time to be creative. We are here to support you, so let's get to work."

The bees quickly and enthusiastically divided up on the sides of the Super Hexagon to get to work in their teams. Each cross-functional group addressed a specific problem.

A roar went up from the Water Team in one corner of the Super Hexagon, but no one seemed to notice as each team was deeply focused on their own topic.

"Wow, this is quite something," commented Queen Leddy as she maneuvered to one of the few open seating areas in the Hexagon. "I love watching these hive hackfests. Look how engaged everyone is," she said to Tanya, the training and development manager and Stella the chief scientist bee.

"I know, the process is amazing to watch," replied Tanya. "In all my years as a professional facilitator, I have to say, this is one of the most effective and efficient ways to solve problems. And it gives everyone a role and ownership in the outcomes."

"I've come to rely on this kind of teamwork. Sometimes I don't feel that I'm needed for anything more than egg laying," said Queen Leddy with a smile.

"Well, that's certainly not the case," added Stella. "You are such an inspiration to the colony. You lead the way in making everyone feel ownership for both the process and the impact our hive is having in the community."

"Speaking of inspiration. Let's wander around and provide some encouragement. I hope they can solve this overheating problem we are having. You know I have been struggling to keep up with laying enough eggs as a result of it being so hot," said Queen Leddy as she wiped the sweat off her brow.

"That's one of the things the Water Team is working on, how to cool the hive with minimal water," responded Tanya. "The drought is putting a strain on our scouts and water foragers as well."

"You can see one of the water problem-solving teams over there to the left side of the Honey Bar. Another is on the other side of the bar. At some point they'll come together."

"Let's have everyone come back together in an hour and hear the recommendations," suggested

Queen Leddy, as she tucked her tail and maneuvered past a few groups to make her way over to one of the water problem-solving teams. Stella and Tanya headed to other parts of the Super Hexagon to listen and offer encouragement.

"What if we were able to use some of the drones during their downtime to become water scouts?" said Holly, a house bee.

"Or, we could scout out the Sunnyvale Farm. That's not far away, and we can see how they are getting water for their animals and crops," added Fleta, the fast flying forager.

"Is there a way for us to store water?" asked Holly. "I know we don't normally store it, that we use it as we bring it in, but I'm wondering if there is a way to turn some of the combs into storage containers. After all, we store honey in them, why not water?"

"Holly, really creative thinking to suggest a way to store water," inserted Stella. "The whole team is doing great, keep up the good work."

"Is there a way we can monitor the water supply and how it is being used to dilute the honey, that way we will know exactly how much we need?" asked Fleta.

"These are great ideas. Our honey supply is at risk if we don't find enough water," replied Eman, an engineering bee.

The bees openly tossed out ideas to explore all the possibilities for finding water sources. No one judged or disparaged another bee's idea. As a cross-functional team, they have a variety of skills and experiences that are helpful in solving problems.

"Maybe we can try all of these ideas," inserted Sabra, the head scout bee. "That way if one doesn't work, we'll know quickly and can then move onto something else. You know, the *fail fast* idea."

"Let's also make sure we are going to have enough bees on stand-by so that when we find the water, they'll be ready to fan it to get the cooling effect going," added Eman.

"Let's make sure we consider the well-being of all the bees," inserted Fleta. "That has to be a key aspect of our solution."

The group eagerly agreed and huddled closer to plan the next steps of their approach to solving the water problem.

"We could take groups out in shifts to hang outside the hive," suggested Wilma the worker bee.

"Wilma, this sounds intriguing. Can you say a bit more about what you have in mind?" encouraged Stella, the chief scientist bee.

"Well, if we can get sizeable enough groups of bees to go outside the hive, then stay outside, for maybe 20 minutes, that could help reduce the temperature inside. That way it's not so crowded in here, and there will be more ventilation."

"Brilliant!" praised Stella. "The queen has been struggling laying eggs because of the heat, and the brood temperature is continuing to rise, threatening this whole brood."

"Do heat waves like this happen often?" asked Iris, a young bee.

"It's hard to say. Each spring and summer now seems to be hotter. Typically it might be hot for a few days then cool off. But the temperature has been hovering close to 100 degrees for the past week. Between the drought and the heat, we're struggling."

"Wilma, would you like to lead the effort to recruit the bees for hanging outside?" asked Stella.

"Glad to help. Let's see how it works. We may need sizeable enough groups to have some impact," replied Wilma excitedly.

"We can get dozens of scouts in each direction to begin the search for new hive locations," offered Betty.

"The foragers can keep an eye out while they are out and report back on anything they see," added Ingrid, a young bee.

"We'll need to carefully calculate the number of swarms and the right types of bees that can safely depart, and still maintain the integrity of the colony," replied Sybil, the head scout.

"This should help with the overheating problem as well," inserted Filia, a forager bee.

"If we got those scouts out in the next hour, they could be back by sundown, and we can hold a massive dance party to see what news they have for new locations," suggested Sybil with a chuckle.

"That would be fun," said Ingrid. "It will be like a giant going away party. Let's break out the mead!"

"But before the fun begins, let's give some thought to how we can cross-train some of the bees so that as their new hives are developing, they'll have enough workers for each task," suggested Filia.

"Let's make a list of all the different types of jobs and see which skills match best," proposed Ingrid. "I'll grab a marker, and we can make the list right here on the yellow board."

A loud whistle could be heard throughout the Super Hexagon. All the bees turned toward the sound, and it was suddenly quiet.

"Let's take another five minutes to have each group finalize your options," announced Tanya. "Then we're going to switch up the teams to do some further review of your best ideas, before we come back together to hear all the proposals. Keep up the great work everyone."

A short time later, Tanya instructed the bees to change groups. Each bee moved to a new problem area, to provide a fresh perspective on the problem at hand.

"Are we ready?" bellowed Queen Leddy. "Time to hear the best of the best ideas. But first, let me say how proud I am of the work you are doing. The collaborative effort I'm seeing here is amazing. You are the best colony in the county!"

A raucous roar went up in the Super Hexagon, as the bees patted each other on the back and high winged each other. After a few minutes they settled down as the idea sharing began.

"Let's have the water team go first," instructed Tanya. "And please, in presenting each idea, include your thoughts on the bee safety and well-being considerations of your proposal."

"On behalf of the water teams, I'm delighted to present these ideas for your consideration," said Eman. "We have a multi-pronged approach to the water problem. First, we are going to convert some of the honeycomb into water storage areas. That way we will have a place to store the water when we find it. In terms of finding the water, we are going to test two concepts simultaneously. That way the teams will be able to compare their results, and we can see which is most effective. The first approach is to visit the Sunnyvale Farm to see how they are watering their animals. The second approach is to cross-train the drones to be water foragers. From a well-being perspective, we recommend bees partner to share sleeping combs, which will let us convert the sleeping combs to water storage combs. We think that bonding in sharing a sleeping comb will deepen the connection between the individual bees."

A cheer went up from the bees as Eman stepped down and Wilma stepped up.

"Thanks so much for your innovative ideas," said Queen Leddy proudly. "Great work."

"I'm next," said Wilma. "We identified that the overheating problem is a result of multiple factors. First, the hive population is at an all-time high, resulting in our self-generated heat. Second, the outside temperatures are affecting us, and third, the lack of water. Our concept for the overheating problem, is to hold daily outside hangouts with groups of bees. This will mean a large group of bees will exit the hive and perch outside nearby. Think of this as a swarm that goes out but doesn't actually leave," she said with a chuckle.

Wilma continued, "This will provide more space for air to circulate, increasing the ventilation. As with so many things we do here, we'll take turns joining the hangouts. During the hangouts, it will be everyone's responsibility to watch out for other bees. At the first sign of fatigue in any bee in the hangout, encourage that bee to return to the hive for a rest break. We don't want anyone to run out of energy. Additionally, we can use the time in the hangouts to get to know each other better, learn about each other's jobs, and have some fun."

Whoops, cheers, and applause could be heard as Wilma stepped down. The final report was from the swarm team.

"On behalf of the swarm team, I'm pleased to share this idea," started Filia. "This one isn't so original, since swarming is a natural part of our existence. What will be different in our approach is the number of scouts we'll send and the different directions they will go. We'll also look to do more swarms than we typically do and carefully select who will go in each swarm. Three things are important in these swarms. First, that we don't lose the culture of our colony. The culture Queen Leddy and the other leaders have created has taught us the importance of our values, teamwork, and communication, and that must not be lost in any of the new hives."

Wild wing applause interrupted Filia's remarks.

"The second point is that our hive makes the best artisanal honey in the county. That attention to detail in selecting nectar and producing our honey is a hallmark of who we are. That also can't be lost in the new hives."

"And finally, we must never forget our purpose, the reason we exist – to keep the planet and its people healthy. We are helping create a world in which everyone eats fruits and vegetables as part of every meal."

The roar was deafening, as the bees stood for a standing ovation. The Super Hexagon was rocking as Filia stepped down and Queen Leddy stepped up again. It took Queen Leddy a few minutes to calm the colony's enthusiasm.

"As always, I'm impressed with the work you do. What a team! I appreciate your enthusiasm but let's not forget that we have a lot of work ahead of us to resolve the current dilemmas." said Queen Leddy respectfully. "So let's get to work and see how this all comes together."

Nancy and Bob
More Differences

Scientist believe that bees may be communicating through electrical fields that build upon their bodies during the course of flying, rubbing, and fluttering.

"I'm fascinated by the contrast in the Alive Hive versus the Dive Hive," started Nancy as she removed her sunglasses. "Fundamentally, they feel so different."

"They are indeed very different," acknowledged Bob as he removed the hat and veil.

"There is such an inherent level of trust and respect among the workers. It is also amazing to see how working in teams changes the culture," continued Nancy. "Everyone, regardless of what team they are on, seems committed to the work not only of their individual group, but how it supports the hive overall."

"Remember, teamwork is one element of the culture. There are many other positive attributes of the culture at play that make the teamwork effective. And you are right. Trust and respect for each other are at the core of much of this. How about all the innovation and creativity that is emerging?" asked Bob.

"That is also intriguing. They are so good at problem-solving and seem so agile to take on the challenges. There is no judgment about right or wrong. The teams are inspired to come up with solutions they think will work. They are empowered to try their ideas, fail fast, and learn from the experience," responded Nancy. "One of the things I also noticed in the Alive Hive is there seems to be a deep one-to-one connection between the bees. They are present for each other in their interactions. We need more presence, agile teamwork, and less hierarchical decision-making. It is the only way we can be nimble and react with the speed we need."

Bob nodded in agreement.

Nancy continued, "It is interesting to see both hives dealing with the same issues, yet taking such different approaches to problem-solving. It is fascinating how the culture supports or diminishes the problem-solving approach."

"Notice anything else?" probed Bob as he stepped out of the sun, into the shade.

"The extent to which the overall health and well-being of the bees is at the core of everything they do. Every single proposal had an embedded element of well-being," answered Nancy. "Look at how taking breaks and sleeping enough positively affects the bees' productivity and demeanor."

"There is a true feeling of being cared for and belonging in the Alive Hive," added Bob.

"So true. I can feel it. This gives me a lot to ponder. I'll be thinking about ways we can instill this in our culture," considered Nancy.

"I have no doubt that you and your team will come up with some really creative solutions," acknowledged Bob. "Let's take a break for lunch and get out of the sun."

"Great idea," agreed Nancy.

Dive Hive
She's Late!

*Swarming is nature's way of reproducing
a hive of bees.*

"She's late!" said Nettie, the Dive Hive nursery bee, fretfully.

"I can see that," responded Nan cantankerously.

"Not just late. Very late." said Nettie nervously

"For the third day in a row," added Nightingale.

"Should we put out the word yet?" asked Nettie, unsure of the timing of sharing news about Queen Cruella.

"Let's wait a little longer to see what happens," encouraged Nightingale. "But we need to keep an eye on this, her production was down every day this past week."

"We can't wait too long or we'll become hopelessly queenless," reminded Nettie. "If she's dying, we need to move or we'll all be dead."

The bees busied themselves with their usual duties preparing for the queen's arrival and her daily egg-laying duties. Meanwhile around them the activities of the nursery continued. Nursing bees feed the hungry pupae, hygienic bees cleaned out the combs of the hatched bees and readied them for the queen to lay more eggs.

"Get out of my way!" commanded Queen Cruella pushing Nettie to the floor, as she arrived in the nursery a full 30 minutes later than usual.

"Yes, your majesty," whimpered Nettie.

"Let's get this over with so I can get back to my throne," instructed Queen Cruella.

The queen's six attending bees busied themselves grooming Queen Cruella by touching her with their mouthparts, antennae, and forelegs. The queen-feeding bees prepared more food in hopes that this would entice her to lay more eggs and keep the hive thriving.

"We've got to get out of this place," sang Wilma, the worker bee.

"Sounds like a song I know," retorted Winter.

"I know you are all excited about the plans, but we need to stay focused," said Whitney, impatiently. "Where do we stand on the swarm plan?"

"The scouts are due back any time," replied Wilma. "As soon as they are back, it will be waggle time to get the word on the locations they have found."

"Good timing, we need to keep this moving. We are running out of time," replied Whitney.

"How is the recruiting going for all the jobs we need?" Whitney probed.

"So far, so good. We've got all the departments covered," replied Winter.

"And how about the queen-to-be?" asked Whitney.

"She will be ready tomorrow," acknowledged Waverly. "Things are looking good on all fronts."

"I'm going to talk with the drones about initiating a few more queens-in-waiting, so we can encourage a few more swarms. Waverly, want to join me?" said Whitney, as she headed off.

"I'm with you," replied Waverly, as she followed Whitney closely.

"Hey guys, have you got a minute to chat?" asked Whitney as she and Waverly entered the drone lounge.

"Absolutely, you know us drones, always hanging out doing nothing," replied Danny with a chuckle. Danny, Dawson, and Doran were lying on soft recliners with their feet up.

"You know things have been bad around here lately," started Whitney.

"I'd have to be dead to not realize that," responded Danny sarcastically.

"Yea, the stress is so much that it is literally killing bees. You heard about Sarge's heart attack didn't you?" replied Dawson.

"I did. Sure is no surprise, given the pace, the stress, the anxiety everyone is feeling," said Whitney. "So you know we need to do something. This is a toxic hive!"

"Good description," responded Doran. "What do you have in mind?"

"That's why we are here. We want to share our plan, and we need your support," added Waverly, and she nodded to Whitney.

"Well, here's the plan. We have a bunch of site scouts out now looking for new hive locations. We expect them back shortly, so we can hear their report, see their dance, and then make a collective decision," replied Whitney, recounting the details of the plan.

"But there is more to it than initiating the swarm. We all know how to do that," continued Waverly. "There needs to be not one, but several swarms. Enough to pretty much abandon this colony. And what will be different from a typical swarm, is we're not taking Queen Cruella with us."

"That's pretty radical and not following with tradition," reacted Danny, turning to see Doran and Dawson's response.

"I know. We've been talking with some of the foragers who've met bees from another hive. They have a very different take on hive operations. And you've seen what's going on here. We have to put an end to the way we are being treated," insisted Whitney.

"How can we help?" asked Dawson.

"Well, let's talk through some of the essentials we want to ensure are in the new hives. Even if we end up splitting up into several hives, we think we can pull this off," continued Waverly.

Whitney chimed in, "You know how overworked everyone is. It doesn't need to be that way. Bees can't go without sleep and rest. That may sound strange to you drones, but the rest of the workers are sleep deprived. We need to create colonies where the well-being of the bees comes first."

"You won't get an argument from us," replied Danny. "We see the exhausted workers in the nursery all the time. They can barely keep their eyes open to clean up the combs and get through the day."

"We also want to initiate some cross-training programs, so that each bee can do multiple jobs," suggested Waverly. "Right now, everyone is comb holed into one job from the day they hatch to the day they die. By having bees who know multiple jobs, we'll be able to work in teams. The teams will be able to switch players at any time to create a new team. This will help with making sure everyone gets enough rest. By not having to do the same boring job their whole life, they will be more engaged, and everyone will get to know each other."

"That's ambitious," pondered Dawson. "But you know, it sounds like a great idea."

"The other big thing is that since we have a new queen, we'll have the opportunity to let her know that we want to do things differently in the new hive," said Whitney.

"We want to make sure everyone feels appreciated and recognized for their contributions. That may be part of the training, to ensure that there is a culture of appreciation and gratitude. And speaking of contributions, this new colony will be about much more than profit," insisted Waverly.

"Well, that'll be a new take on things," said Doran sarcastically.

"It has to be," said Whitney passionately. "Look at all the good we do in this county with our pollination and honey production. Profit is *not* a reason for being, it is a side benefit, an outcome."

"We'll also have leaders in the new hive, but they will be very different than the leaders here," added Waverly. "These leaders will work well together as a team. They will complement each other. They will also be good coaches and be supportive of the worker teams. They will encourage experimenting and taking risks. And they will listen and communicate rather than live isolated in their ivory comb tower."

"So what do you think? Does it sound like a good plan? Are you with us?" asked Whitney.

"Count us in!" responded Doran, Dawson, and Danny in unison.

"They're here, they're here!" exclaimed Goldie, the guard bee.

"Spread the word, so everyone can hear the news," instructed Gjerta.

"We're so excited about what we found," said Sammy the scout bee breathlessly.

"Are we ready?" asked Samantha. "May the best sites win!"

The mass of bees gathered where they could see the nest-site scouts as they started the waggle dance. The furious movements in the figure-eight dance were dizzying. Dozens of nest-site scout bees danced to tell their story of the sites they found for the new hive locations. The vibration level in the hive was astounding as bees buzzed with giddy excitement.

The waggle dance is a debate showing the characteristics and strengths of the various site options. As the strengths emerge, the bees supporting that particular site, moved toward the nest-site scout to show their support. The waggle dance continued until the final two locations were being debated.

"It looks like we have a consensus," remarked Whitney as a cheer went up.

"See, that's the type of teamwork we want to have in our new colonies," added Waverly.

"It's impressive to see the democratic process at work with so many bees having their say in the decision," added Dawson.

Nancy and Bob Abandon Ship!

Worker bees notice a lower level of phero-mone secreted by a queen when she is too old or sick and prepare special honeycomb cells for the birth of a new queen.

"**A**bandon ship," teased Nancy as she took a drink of water on this warm afternoon near the hives.

"That's about right," acknowledged Bob with a chuckle.

"Queen Cruella is so self-centered and clueless about what is going on around her. It's as if she thinks all the bees are there to serve her," said Nancy.

"Apparently she missed the leadership class on being a servant leader," added Bob, with a wry smile on this face.

"What is interesting, is seeing that a few workers are stepping up and taking the lead, since there is a leadership vacuum," commented Nancy.

"At this point, it seems to be a matter of survival. The bees recognized that they couldn't keep working this way, so they are taking action," replied Bob.

"But in the real world, a whole workforce wouldn't abandon the hive, would they?" said Nancy.

"It happens, especially in today's world where barriers to entry are so low. It's possible for a few key people to walk away and start their own, competing business. That way they can shape the organization the way they want, and create a culture that suits the people they want to attract," replied Bob.

"Actually, now that I think about it, that is exactly what happened in a firm that I worked for early in my career. It was even harder to do then, without all the technology we have today. But the group that left went on to create a thriving business," responded Nancy thoughtfully. "Many more people left right after they departed. Not quite the mass swarm exit that we are seeing here."

"Remember, employees vote with their feet. When the economy is good, they will look for the employer that is going to offer them the flexibility, autonomy, culture, and benefits that employees want these days," said Bob.

"There are so many moving parts to have in alignment to make a workplace a truly thriving hive," said Nancy thoughtfully.

"You are right about that. And when you get it right, it is oh, so wonderful," replied Bob. "What's missing in the Dive Hive is at the core; they don't care about the worker bees. When that is missing, the rest doesn't matter."

"Didn't someone famous once say "If you take care of your employees, they will take care of everything else," said Nancy chuckling.

Bob laughed. "Yes, something like that."

Reflection Questions

Take a few minutes as Nancy did to reflect on how your organization resembles the Dive Hive and the Alive Hive. Use these questions as a guide in your reflection.

Your Organization

- To what extent does your organization's culture support teamwork during stressful times?
- When there are threats or times of stress in your business, how does the team pull together or does it become fragmented?
- To what extent are employees empowered to make decisions that are right for the business?
- To what extent is there transparency in communications that support decision-making?

Managing Oneself

- To what extent is employee well-being compromised for the greater good of the organization?
- How do taking breaks, getting enough sleep and being rested support your personal goals? Your organization's goals?

- What personal habits and rituals support your being your best self? Are there any missing that you can start doing?

Alive Hive
Innovation at Work

Swarms send out a few hundred scouts to locate and evaluate new nest sites.

"This is brilliant," said Tanya as she walked through the comb area of the Alive Hive now being used for water storage. "I can't believe someone didn't think of this before."

"I know, it is pretty amazing," replied Eman. "Our team is really proud of this solution."

"Rightfully so," acknowledged Wendy, a water bee just returning with more water. "It may be the solution we need to keep our honey quality high. We were able to spy – okay, not exactly spying – on Sunnyvale Farm to see how they are watering their animals and found some water troughs where we can hang out to get water."

Wendy passed the water to Henna, a hygienic bee who has been cross-trained to be a water storage bee. Henna put the water in the comb and sealed it to store the water.

"That was also great thinking," said Tanya. "After all, Sunnyvale is the largest farm in the county. You knew they would have a way of dealing with the drought. And how is the drone cross-training going?"

"That's going well also. They aren't used to flying long distances, since they normally just go a short distance from the hive. But they are taking on flying longer distances as a challenge and having some fun with it," replied Eman.

"You should see the leader board they added to the HON Board to show how far each drone is flying daily," added Henna with a hoot.

"Leave it to the guys to make a challenge out of everything," chuckled Wendy.

"It definitely seems cooler in here already," said Queen Leddy as she entered the nursery to resume her daily egg laying. "What's the secret to your success?"

"The dual approach experiment is paying off," replied Nova, a nursery bee. "The outside hangouts are a big hit. It is especially popular with the inside worker bees who don't usually leave the hive. They think this is the best thing ever."

"It is amazing to see the reaction from the inside bees the first time they go out. They get excited beyond words," added Noelle. "And when they come back into work at their regular jobs, they have much more energy."

"Maybe we should make outside hangouts a regular part of everyone's job," suggested Queen Leddy. "Were there any fatigue issues? It's still pretty hot out there."

"Actually, none," replied Nova. "Everyone was trained on symptoms of heat fatigue prior to going out. At the first sign of any bees stressing from the heat, they were escorted back inside to rest."

"Well, everything sounds under control," said Queen Leddy confidently. "I knew that the teams would come up with great solutions."

Queen Leddy continued, "Now it's my turn to get back to work here. I understand we need a few new queens-in-waiting for the upcoming swarm."

"You are correct," acknowledged Noelle. "The swarms are planned for next week. You can see the twenty wax queen cells over here."

Noelle directed Queen Leddy to the cells containing the queen larvae. The young nurse bees have been feeding them the rich, creamy royal jelly for several days.

"I'm hoping to have some time with them before our swarm departs to tell them about our purpose in the community and the world," said Queen Leddy.

"Carrying on the traditions and values we've established in this colony will get them started on a good path," acknowledged Nova. "We'll keep you posted on their development."

"Are there any questions?" asked Stella, the chief scientist bee, as she looked out over the hundreds of bees before her. Stella is finishing up cross-training for bees that will be departing in the upcoming swarms.

"I have one," replied Willow, a newly trained pollen-processing bee. "Do I understand correctly that the quality of the honey is directly related to the water content?"

"Great question, Willow," replied Stella patiently. "I know this is a hard concept to get, and it is so important to your being able to produce the same high quality artisanal honey in the new hive colonies. So let's take this slowly to ensure you all feel confident with this explanation. Jump in with questions anytime."

Stella continued with the lesson. "Remember, there are many aspects that impact the quality of honey, including: moisture levels, debris, bubbles, wax flakes, and foam. That's one of the many reasons that our hygienic bees keep the hive clean. And of course, the taste of the honey is a key factor. There can't be any peculiar flavors picked up during processing.

"The water content is especially important. In processing, you want to be capping the combs when the water content reaches 17 to 18 percent. If the water content gets higher than that, there is a possibility that the honey will ferment," added Stella.

"Thank you," acknowledged Willow. "That is very clear."

"We'll have a few more days for all of you to work here to observe the pollen processing. I trust that you'll all do a great job in your new hives. But remember, I can always come visit to see how your honey tastes," teased Stella.

"What a raucous blowout," yelled Holly, the house bee as she stood inside the Super Hexagon.

"It sure is. These bees sure know how to party," replied Henna, as she moved to the Honey Bar for a drink. "One thing we know in this: hive celebration boosts everyone's positive outlook and feeling a part of the hive's accomplishments."

"No one seems the least bit upset that the swarm is happening tomorrow," commented Hope to her buddy Heather.

"Why would they be?" asked Heather. "We are all family, and we are all well trained for our jobs in the new hives. There's nothing to be upset about."

"I guess you're right," responded Hope. "And since we now do outside hangouts, we can visit each other when we are on a rest break."

Nancy and Bob
Any Surprises?

Artisanal honey comes from one location and includes harvesting nectar from a mix of flowers and flowering trees.

"Did it turn out the way you expected?" asked Bob as he and Nancy sat in the shade under a tree near the hives.

Nancy paused for a moment as she looked up at the cloudless, cerulean sky. "Well, yes. I expected that with all the good planning and teamwork that the bees in the Alive Hive would succeed. They came up with creative solutions, experimented, and executed to create a great outcome," replied Nancy.

"The supportive environment they created led to that success," noted Bob.

"I totally agree. The bees are actively engaged in decision-making, are empowered, and have autonomy. That supportive environment appears to come from shared values that are at play. The sense of respect, trust, and integrity drive their actions," acknowledged Nancy.

"You nailed it. Shared values are essential to the culture that cares for people. Whether that is the worker bees, the customers, all stakeholders," acknowledged Bob enthusiastically.

"What I also see in play here is communication. There is transparency about what is going on in the organization, where they are headed, and why," added Nancy.

"Communications is such a critical piece to the puzzle," replied Bob. "I think I've had my share of lessons learned on this front over the years. I thought it was better to share information on a need to know basis and keep bad news from people. I learned that the more open and honest you can be, the less stressed they are. Everyone playing a guessing game about what is going on is a complete waste of time and energy. Sharing information is a big piece of where the trust element comes into play."

"I also noticed that they don't take themselves so seriously. How about that raucous party?" asked Nancy with a smile.

"I'm the first to admit, that sometimes we need to lighten up and have some fun," agreed Bob with a loud laugh. "Adding celebrations and fun to any organization is going to have lasting impact."

Dive Hive
Swarm for Change

Swarm bees stay inactive and consume honey when preparing to swarm.

"Sure is quiet around here," said Faith, a forager bee, noticing the stillness in the Dive Hive upon returning from her most recent flight.

"What a contrast to the normal buzz," replied Fiona, looking around. "Something's up."

"What do you mean?" asked Fannie curiously.

"I bet this is the what they call the 'calm before the swarm,' when everyone is fattening up on honey for the flight to the new colony. Let's look around. I'll bet we see a bunch of bloated bees lying around, too stuffed to even move," said Fiona.

"Look!" exclaimed Fannie as she pointed to a cluster of bees lying in the corner of a comb. They are so lethargic and puffy, they can barely move.

"And there, they have tabs of beeswax in their wax gland," directed Fiona. "Sure enough, it must be about time for the swarm. They will use that wax to build the honeycomb in the new hive."

"Everything ready?" asked Gjerta, the guard bee, as she stood near the edge of the hive, as Goldie looked on.

"Looks like we are ready to roll," replied Whitney, enthusiastically.

"We've got all the preparations made," confirmed Waverly.

"Gjerta, stand back. This is going to take a while, and there will be a massive swarm, since we've got two groups heading out," instructed Whitney.

"I'll remind everyone to stay calm," inserted Goldie. "Swarming is pretty chaotic, with everyone being stuffed with honey and wax."

"I can't wait to hear how it all goes," replied Gjerta supportively. "You've done everything right in terms of building consensus with the worker bees on the new hives. It is bound to be a success. And, I'll be on guard here making sure that only healthy bees go with you. Anyone that has mites or disease will be held back."

"You're the best," said Waverly.

"Off we go!" said Whitney and Waverly in harmony.

Suddenly, thousands of bees burst out of the hive in unison. There was significant commotion as the bees headed toward the new hive locations. The majority of the bees settled high up on the outside of an old American chestnut, where the massive swarm waited as the comb construction was underway inside the tree cavity. The other swarm headed further north, where they settled in a large elm tree.

"Stack them up over here, please" instructed Charlene, the comb construction group leader, to the comb building workers as they piled up the beeswax to build the hexagon combs.

"How much do we need?" asked Candy, another of the comb building squad.

"We've got a ways to go," replied Charlene. "This is an enormous swarm, and we'll need room for everyone."

"This is such a great location," commented Wanda, as she hung out with the swarm waiting for the hive to be ready to occupy.

"Look at those lovely trees for a northerly wind break," replied Wilma. "I think I'm going to like living here."

"I know, look at the downward slope of the land away from the trees," added Wanda. "That will provide for such nice airflow away from the colony. It seems like heaven already! The nest-scout bees did a great job finding this spot."

"And look over there," gasped Wendy. "We can see the other swarm, they are in that giant elm tree. See them, right near the top."

"Look at that. It's great to know our sisters are close by," answered Wilma. "But I do feel bad for Queen Cruella, Benny, Sarge, and Kindra. I hope Sarge is going to be okay."

"I'm confident Sarge will make a speedy recovery. Now, let's pay attention here," reminded Wanda. "We need to keep the swarm core temperature as constant as we can, while we are waiting for the initial comb construction to be completed."

"We want to be sure some of the swarm core gets a chance to rest while we keep them cool," added Wendy. "Remember, conserving our energy is an important part of our new colony. No more brow beating to exhaustion by Queen Cruella."

"This is a pretty swanky place," commented Doran as he looked around the new drone lounge.

"I think we are going to like it here," added Dawson, settling into a lounge chair.

"Don't get too comfortable just yet," inserted Danny. "As soon as things settle down here, we're heading out to meet the virgin queen. Time to get to work on populating this new colony."

"Can you feel it? Doesn't it already feel different?" asked Doran.

"Yes, I can feel it. Did you see how the teams are working together on the comb construction and keeping the swarm temperature under control? The teams are happily buzzing," sighed Dawson.

"This is exactly the kind of place I've always wanted to work," said Danny as he closed his eyes for a short nap.

"This is different than what I'm used to," said Petunia, the pollen processing bee, as she lifted a ladle of honey from the tub.

"Have we done something wrong?" inquired Pamela as she looked on.

"No, this is the way honey is supposed to be," answered Penelope. "What's different here is that we're not trying to make massive quantities of honey as we did for Queen Cruella. All she wanted was quantity, not quality."

"Right, all she cared about was profit," rejoined Petunia.

"When you have just the right amount of water in the honey, it is smooth, fragrant, and has a silky texture," added Pillar, the more senior of the pollen processing bees.

"What we're making here is a finer quality of honey," replied Penelope. "This will sell far better at the farmers market.

"It seems so different to focus on quality of the honey, not the mass production of a low-quality honey," said Petunia. "I think everyone is going to feel great pride in this product. We most certainly never felt that way with Sarge standing over us and Queen Cruella driving us to death with quotas."

"Thanks so much for volunteering for this team," said Wanda, a worker bee and team lead on the Well-being Ambassador Network. "The role you've signed up for will contribute significantly to the well-being of our individual bees and the colony as a whole."

Wanda looked out at the hundreds of bees who had volunteered to be part of this important network. At the core of this colony's values is the well-being of all the bees. The Ambassador Network is an approach to helping the colony keep tabs on the needs of the workers and communicating those needs

"Before we get started with the details, let's take a few minutes to be present in the moment, to focus on our intentions of our work, and to be grateful for our sisters and brothers in our colony," added Wyn, a worker bee well known for her calming presence, as she guided the bees in a moment of silence.

"Today, we will focus on the basics of your role as a well-being ambassador, how we will communicate and share ideas," Wanda continued.

The worker bees are keenly focused as Wanda and Wyn explained their well-being ambassador role, encouraging them to talk with their fellow bees regularly about what is working, not working, and what we can do differently in the hive. The ambassadors meet weekly to share what they hear and develop action plans to address any issue that is compromising bee safety and well-being. The Ambassador Network plays a key role in the communications of the hive to ensure everything is working, and that all bees feel supported and safe.

"Welcome to the nursery, Queen Alicia," said Nina, the nursery bee, warmly as the queen entered the nursery for the first time.

A dozen bees suddenly moved to Queen Alicia's side. "Thanks so much for the warm welcome," said Queen Alicia, feeling embraced by the workers with a sense of belonging.

"We've been anticipating your arrival," said Nadia. "There are many steps to prepare the comb for eggs, but we have a great team, and they all worked together."

"Well, I'm delighted to hear that, and grateful for the great work everyone has done together with the preparations. After all, without your work, my egg laying would be for naught," said Queen Alicia thankfully.

A small cheer erupted from the nursery bees, as they gave each other high wings. They felt good knowing that Queen Alicia appreciated the role they played in the hive.

"At the end of the week, let's plan a field trip to the summer carnival," suggested Queen Alicia. "It will be fun to get out of the hive and play a little." The bees were abuzz in anticipation of the outing with the queen and the chance to socialize.

"We've got a lot of work to do here to get this brood going and to keep this hive thriving. I was with the drones yesterday, so I'm ready any time you are," invited Queen Alicia. "Shall we get started?"

"Is everyone ready?" encouraged Nadia, as the bees prepared the queen for egg laying.

"What's happening here?" demanded Queen Cruella as she wandered around the hive for the first time in weeks. She encountered Benny, Sarge, and Kindra standing in the comb hallway.

"You missed it," responded Benny. "You should get out more. We've experienced a massive swarm. Actually, multiple swarms. The colony is pretty much cleaned out."

"How can that be?" asked Queen Cruella incredulously.

"Well, I know this is hard to hear, but the reason they gave for leaving was how fed up they were feeling stressed and exhausted," offered Kindra honestly, "not to mention unappreciated."

"Why I gave them my all! I used every ounce of effort at my command encouraging them to do more, go further, strive harder," replied Queen Cruella.

"While making our numbers was important to you, the talk around the hive was it came at the expense of too much that was important to them," added Sarge, looking healthier than he had in ages.

"What can be more important than profit?" asked Queen Cruella looking baffled.

"Lots of things," countered Kindra. "The well-being of the worker bees for one. You can never achieve your business objectives if the worker bees are burned out."

"Maybe if you had acknowledged they were part of something bigger," inserted Benny.

"What would that be?" asked Queen Cruella, looking very annoyed.

"For one thing, you could have acknowledged that their daily work served a bigger purpose, such as the importance of pollination and the impact that has for the environment," replied Kindra.

"And, creating a work environment where people feel cared for, where they have a sense of belonging, and where they can create meaningful relationships with their fellow worker bees," added Sarge. "I've come to appreciate this much more since I had my heart attack. It's not about working hard every day. Relationships make working mean something."

"And where were you, my trusted advisors when all of this was going on?" Asked Queen Cruella. "Humph! I should ban you from the colony." She sighed looking lost and hopeless. "If they've all left, what will happen to us now?"

"They've left us a core crew and enough honey to get through the winter," replied Sarge.

"We can rebuild this colony to create a thriving hive, or give up right now," offered Kindra. "It is your choice."

Nancy and Bob
Compare and Contrast

When the first replacement queen emerges from her cell, she immediately stings the remaining developing queens' cells. When two emerge simultaneously they fight to the death.

"This is such a contrast to where the Dive Hive started," said Nancy as she and Bob began their walk back to the house, carrying their veiled helmets. Bailey trailed closely behind them.

"I agree. It feels like it will be a place where the bees are honored and respected for the work they do," agreed Bob. "And the bees aren't all stressed and exhausted."

"The teamwork is really developing which, as we have seen, is essential to a thriving organization," added Nancy.

"But it was also how the bees could see that when taking the lead, rather than waiting for someone to tell them what to do, they made good decisions. They accomplished a lot more. The power of autonomy and purpose," said Bob.

"When the bees are actively engaged in the decision-making, they feel ownership," acknowledged Nancy.

"What about the peer support?" asked Bob.

"That's another key aspect that I appreciate," said Nancy. "When the peers shared their knowledge and experience, it provided that supportive environment in which everyone succeeded."

"Do you think you can teach old bees new tricks?" asked Bob with a smile.

"You mean Queen Cruella and her crew? I think they see that it is a matter of survival. You have to change and grow in order to survive," said Nancy.

Alive Hive
Swarm for Growth

A swarm is made up of as many as 20,000 bees and one queen.

"**W**ell, it is time," said Sabra, the head scout bee.

"Looks like everyone is ready," responded Fleta, the forager bee.

"I'm sad to leave my daughters behind in the Alive Hive and watch others leave in their own swarm. But I'm confident that they will create thriving hives, that they will impact many lives through the flowers, fruit, and vegetables they pollinate, and they will live happily ever after," said Queen Leddy with a tear in her eye.

"No need to be sad," encouraged Sabra. "Everyone will be close by. We can hang out together when the bees come out of their hive to cool it down."

Moments later, thousands of bees burst forth from the hive as the swarms began. Queen Leddy was in the first swarm to depart, as is tradition. The swarms landed high on trees near the lake where there is good airflow. They hoped that the drought would end soon and the water levels would again rise to normal.

"This way gang," cheered Sandy the scout. "Let's get this hive built and populated."

"The comb construction teams need to head in first so they can get started," directed Phenicia, the lead pollen processing bee. "Once we get the core structure in place, we can get the Super Hexagon built."

"Phenicia, can you spare some workers for the nursery area?" inquired Nina, the nursery bee.

"Absolutely, whatever you need," offered Phenicia. "No reason we can't build the nursery at the same time as the pollen storage areas. Take this crew with you and show them where you want them to get started."

"Grateful for your support and the team work," replied Nina, as she headed to the area where the new nursery would be constructed.

Meanwhile, outside the hive, the bees were hanging in their swarm as they waited for the hive construction to commence. In the interest of keeping preparations moving, the communications, engineering, and technology team were busy planning the new HON Board.

"Ready for some hoopla?" asked Tina, a technology bee. Hoopla is the process the bees use when finishing up on a project or starting a new project. They ask three questions: what worked, what didn't work, what should we do differently.

"Let's review all the things that worked really well with the last HON Board," suggested Edith, a member of the engineering squad. "That way we can be sure to keep the best of what worked."

"It was easy for everyone to see, where it was located in the Super Hexagon," suggested Eve. "Everyone has the right information at the right time. The location and the visibility of the HON Board is key for that."

"Spoken like a true engineer," joked Tabatha, of the technology team.

"The information that was on the board worked well," inserted Carmen, of the communications group. "We had all the forager flight stats, the brood counts at each stage of development, and all the info on the pollen processing."

"One thing that didn't work was that everyone has to come to the Super Hexagon to see the board. Perhaps we can find a way to do mini-HON Boards in other locations throughout the hive. That way bees don't need to leave their work areas to get the information," suggested Eman.

"Eman, that is a good suggestion. We have to remember that the reason we wanted worker bees to step away from their work area and come to the

Super Hexagon is to take a break and to interact with bees from other departments," added Esther.

"Good point Esther," reflected Eman. "I had forgotten that was part of the reason for building the HON Board in the first place. We wanted not only a great way for everyone to have access to all the right data at the right time, but we wanted to encourage them to look after their own well-being and to connect with other bees. Some of these jobs are stressful, taking a break is reinvigorating."

"Maybe we should do a quick poll of the worker bees and see if they feel mini-HON Boards would be helpful. Maybe there is critical time-sensitive information." returned Cindy. "We get such useful ideas each time we ask the bees what works best for them."

"We can ask them for additional suggestions that we can use as well," added Carmen. "You know how vocal these bees are. They've always got great suggestions."

"What else should we be doing differently?" asked Edith, guiding the conversation to the next step.

There was a minute of silence, as the bees contemplated the HON Board functionality.

"I know," piped in Tina. "What if we add a section to the board that features every bee having a birthday that day. That way, everyone who sees the birthday bees can wish them a happy birthday. Think how much that will make each bee feel like they belong."

Applause erupted from the bees for Tina's idea.

"Are the troops ready to go?" asked Queen Leddy, as she stood in the Super Hexagon.

"They are," replied Sabra, the scout bee. "This is going to be such fun."

"I know, it is one of my favorite times of the week," responded Queen Leddy.

"Same for me," countered Sabra joyfully.

This Friday is a special day, as Queen Leddy and a quarter of the colony headed out to the county fair. Each Friday is outing day, but the county fair only happens one time each summer. This excursion gave the bees a chance to step away from their work, to get to know bees from other work areas, and most importantly, to have fun.

"I like taking a break as much as anyone. Sorry to sound skeptical, Sabra, but given how important our pollen processing is, how can we take that much time off and take the other workers off their jobs each week, too?" asked Patty.

"Watch," encouraged Sabra. "You'll see how it works. Let's have some fun."

"Whoever came up with this idea is brilliant," said Hedda, a hygienic bee about to head out from the hive. "I never get to go outside so this is a real treat for me."

"I feel the same way," said Nina, the nursery bee as she joined Hedda for the outing. "I get to meet so many other bees when we do this."

Hundreds of bees followed them out of the hive as they headed to the county fair.

"Wheee, I'm flying so fast," said Cindy as she flitted along soaring above the ground.

"This is the best," added Eman, as she flew along with Cindy.

As the sun was setting, the bees headed back to the hive, ecstatic, exuberant, and exhausted from the outing. All had fun as they explored the county fair. Soda and juice cans in the trash bins were a bounty of sweetness. Other bees were beside themselves with joy when they found discarded cotton candy on the ground.

"Esther, it was such fun to hang out with you today," said Tabatha a technology bee.

"Likewise," said Hedda, "so glad we got to meet. If there is ever any clean up you need, let me know. I'm an expert at clean up."

"Will do," acknowledged Tabatha.

"So, how was your time at the fair, Patty?" asked Sabra as she hovered just outside the hive watching the bees returning.

"Now I get it," said Patty enthusiastically to Sabra, no longer feeling skeptical. "I can see how energized and refreshed everyone is. Stepping away for a while, is invigorating. And I got to meet a whole bunch of bees that I never would have met otherwise."

"This is the best I've ever tasted," chirped Phenicia, as she slurped the latest batch of artisanal honey.

"It is such a scrumptious flavor, if I say so myself," said Patty proudly as she looked over Phenicia's wing.

"I think this will definitely win the blue ribbon at the county fair," encouraged Prudence.

"Wouldn't that be fabulous," replied Phenicia enthusiastically. "Look at how clear and smooth it is. We'll have to be sure to thank the hygienic bees for their great work on keeping the combs so clean. We want to make sure they know how their work contributes to our hive's success and our soon-to-be prize-winning honey."

"It is so rewarding that we have been able to carry on the traditions and quality of our honey products in our new colony," added Patty. "All that cross-training and teamwork is paying off."

"We sure have a good thing going here," sighed Prudence contentedly. "This is definitely a thriving hive!"

Epilogue

"A world without bees would be almost impossible to contemplate and likely one in which we would never have evolved in the first place."

– Mark L. Winston
Bee Time

Nancy waved to Bob from across the restaurant. Six months had passed since their last visit. She had arrived a few minutes early, eagerly awaiting Bob's arrival.

"Bob, welcome. I'm delighted that we could make this time work to get together," said Nancy enthusiastically.

"As am I. This time fit perfectly between a few meetings I'm in town for today," answered Bob. "I've missed our conversations and our time with the hives."

"Likewise. Tell me, how are the hives doing?" asked Nancy.

"Ah! They are all tucked away for the winter. I hope this year isn't too harsh weather-wise, so they have enough honey to get through. I will check them periodically and supplement their reserves if needed," replied Bob.

"I so appreciate the time we spent together this spring and summer. It was such an interesting learning experience. One I can honestly say was completely unexpected," said Nancy.

"I agree that it wasn't quite the place that I expected to learn some of these lessons. But it sure is fascinating," acknowledged Bob encouragingly.

"I want to share with you how I've used what I learned and what I've been doing over the past few months," said Nancy. "But first, let's order lunch."

"Can't wait to hear!" encouraged Bob.

Just then the waiter stopped by to take Nancy and Bob's lunch order.

"I have some news and a gift for you," said Bob as he handed Nancy a small bag.

"What's this?" asked Nancy curiously looking into the bag.

"My honey won a first prize in the artisanal honey category at the State Fair," announced Bob. "I thought you'd like a bottle as a memento."

"Wow, thank you, and congratulations! That's quite an accomplishment," exclaimed Nancy.

"It is indeed. There was very steep competition from beekeepers that have been doing this a lot longer than I have," said Bob proudly.

"I know I'll enjoy the honey. Maybe you'll even share the recipe for those fabulous honey cakes," joked Nancy with a nudge of her elbow toward Bob.

"So tell me, how did the Cross-County Trek ride turn out. I was disappointed that it conflicted with my niece's wedding," asked Bob.

"It was a huge hit. We picked up a few more employees and family members to ride. The number of volunteers was almost double over what we first recruited. We're going to make this an annual event," smiled Nancy. "Not only do I feel more fit from training for the ride, the connection to the team was fabulous. And the connection to the community was so heartfelt."

"Wonderful. I'll definitely want to be part of it next year," responded Bob. "So tell me, how have you been applying the lessons from the hives?"

"As we talked about after my first visit, I spent much more time walking around, being visible. I could see that this had an immediate impact. It brought me much closer to the operations but also more in touch with the people. I think they began to get to know me and see who I am as a person," started Nancy.

"Those connections are so valuable. So often leaders are aloof and inaccessible. And while you may have many super powers, you are still a human being. I think when people see us for who we are, then we become much more approachable," suggested Bob.

"I came to appreciate that in order to engage our employees, we need to understand what motivates them. We've established regular meetings where everyone gets to share their ideas and interests, and we've tried to make it a very open and safe environment. I've found having both formal and informal ways to get input from the employees gives them ways they feel most comfortable giving me information. After gathering enough ideas and inventorying them, we ask everyone to vote on what's most important to them. Some of these ideas have been easy wins," continued Nancy.

"Give me an example of an easy win," prompted Bob.

"Employees wanted healthier foods in the workplace. They pushed us to replace some of the junk food vending machines," stated Nancy.

"Hard to argue with that," acknowledged Bob.

"Perhaps the biggest lesson I saw in the hives, was the extent to which we need to take care of our employees and their well-being," continued Nancy. "This is by far my biggest take-away."

"I know. It is so fundamental, and yet many leaders forget they can't achieve their business objectives without them. And with them healthy and happy, they'll perform more efficiently and effectively," responded Bob.

"I used this idea to start some new initiatives and to refresh some old programs. For example, we used to have all kinds of recognition programs. With changes in our Human Resource leaders over the years, some of those fell by the wayside. I'm working with the HR team to bring some of those back," continued Nancy.

"How has that been received?" asked Bob curiously.

"The employees love it. They've even come up with some of their own recognition ideas," replied Nancy. "The employees suggested a program we are calling We Care. Employees can nominate a peer when they observe them doing something that demonstrates the core values of the organization. It can be something nice they did for a customer or for another employee. The stories are so heartwarming and creating a culture of gratitude that is deepening the connection we have with each other."

Nancy paused as the waiter served them their lunch entrees.

"Anything else I can bring right now?" asked the waiter.

"Thank you. I think we are all set," replied Nancy.

"The other thing that we did is hire a business school classmate of mine, who is a specialist in employee well-being, she has been conducting focus groups with employees to get their input on a variety of topics. Having an outside professional facilitate these focus groups, let employees know that they could speak openly and honestly. Also, I loved that hoopla idea, of asking what is working, not working, or can be done differently," continued Nancy.

"I love that idea also. How's it working?" asked Bob.

"Something so simple and yet we've gathered a lot of great information. Some ideas are way out there, but that's to be expected in a free-wheeling brainstorming session. Just getting people into conversation helps bring out what they want and value most," said Nancy.

"I'm in total agreement on that. Conversation is becoming a lost art, given everyone's preoccupation with technology. Call me a dinosaur, but for me there is nothing like a good long conversation to help make a connection with a person," added Bob.

"No one would call you a dinosaur," acknowledged Nancy with a chuckle. "I totally agree about the importance of communications. And that's another aspect of what we are changing. We are rebuilding sizable areas of our office space to provide more places where employees can congregate for informal socialization and conversations. We're also creating workspaces, where groups have their own area for collaborating," said Nancy enthusiastically.

"Gone are the days of the cubicle farms?" asked Bob with a laugh.

"Long gone," acknowledged Nancy. "It's been interesting as we begin to get the input from the employees, how they seem much more engaged.

"We haven't looked at our benefits programs in a long time. It was way overdue for a full makeover. The demographics of our workforce have changed a lot in the last few years. As you know, we've had a very rich benefits package for years, with lots of great financial benefits, wellness programs, and the like. We decided to let the employees prioritize which benefits they value most. We were surprised by the results."

"What a great idea. What is important for them?" Bob queried.

"You'll love this. The top benefit that employees wanted was doggie day care," Nancy said with a laugh. "The second priority was flexible work schedules."

"What fun. So now everyone will bring their dogs to work?" asked Bob with a chuckle. "Bailey would love that!"

"Well, not exactly. We are going to repurpose an area within our building to add this benefit. That way employees can take breaks and walk their dogs. Or if they are doing a walking meeting they can get their dog and take their dog along. We are also definitely encouraging more breaks. That's part of the feedback we got from the focus groups. Employees felt really stressed, and so much so they didn't have time to take breaks, even for lunch most days," said Nancy.

"Stress is something we used to accept as part of the job. Now that we know how damaging it is to our health, we know getting a handle on it improves not only individual health but the health of the organization," acknowledged Bob.

"You're right. This was a clear case of us not listening. Stress has shown up on the employee engagement surveys for the past couple of years. But this time, we're listening. We are implementing programs that will help manage stress, such as mindfulness and exercise programs. But more importantly we are engaging with work groups to understand the sources of stress. Job design is one possible source: are we asking people to do too much; do they have all the tools they need to do their job? By designing the job with their well-being in mind, it has done a lot to increase their engagement and reduce their stress. Another problem we're solving is the excessive amount of email."

"Has the team come up with creative solutions for that issue?" asked Bob.

"I've been amazed by the creativity and willingness to try new things. We implemented a collaboration software program that has already cut down on the amount of email we've all been getting. It's rewarding to see the results of these changes taking place," said Nancy.

"Leaving that creativity untapped can be frustrating for employees. You've clearly gone about unleashing it the right way. And if everyone is as enthusiastic as you are, it will no doubt be a success," encouraged Bob.

"I've learned so much in thinking about well-being. What a broad topic. It encompasses so much of who we are as individuals and what helps us thrive. We've embraced it as a core value, just as the Alive Hive did. We are doing a systemic review so that it is part of everything we do." Nancy paused to take a drink of water, and then continued.

"There are a couple of other things that we are doing. We are focused on doing a better job of articulating our purpose and vision for a better world. Our products impact our customers' lives in such an important way. We are working to make that connection for our employees. Starting to do this right at the beginning of the hiring process, assures us that when someone joins us, they are passionate about the work we are doing.

"We're seeing that connecting to our purpose inspires people. And we're connecting purpose to the core values of the company. Purpose linked to values gives us concrete guiding principles of who we are and how we are going to get there. Seeing the renewed engagement shows that employees are responding to the alignment with a strong purpose."

"That appeals to the millennials, for sure, and goes well beyond what we imagined was important for motivating employees," replied Bob. "You're smart to have that alignment from the start."

"But one of the things I'm having the most fun with is bowling," said Nancy.

"Bowling?" asked Bob, with a puzzled look on his face.

"Yes, remember the fun the Alive Hive had on their outings? I thought we would give that a try." She paused. "I never could have imagined the impact this would have."

"Bowling?" repeated Bob.

"Remember that bowling alley a few blocks from the office?" asked Nancy.

"Sure," replied Bob. "It's been there forever."

"Every Friday, we take a quarter of the employees bowling. We play a couple of games for an hour and a half. They have three-person teams, so they meet new people each time. Over a 12-week period, they have met about 20 to 30 other people in the company that they might not have met otherwise. It has been a huge hit," said Nancy with a smile. "It is heartwarming to see how this has created a sense of community and making people feel that they belong. They get to know each other beyond their jobs and build meaningful relationships. And we have fun."

"That does sound like fun. And it is moving to hear that you're seeing the impact in the way people are connecting," suggested Bob.

"Well, I'm glad that it is working out. I have to tell you. This has been an exercise in planned experimentation. We arrived at the bowling solution after a false start on a different approach," explained Nancy. "At first we were having an afternoon happy hour on Thursdays around five o'clock. You may know that craft beers are all the rage now. So we set up a kegerator with some of the local craft beers on tap."

"Is that what it's really called?" asked Bob with a chuckle.

"Yes, a kegerator. Anyway, at first it was a big hit. Everyone was having fun and it even became the day of the week some of the people who telecommute started coming into the office," said Nancy.

"All sounds good so far," added Bob.

"We thought so as well. Remember the stress topic we discussed earlier? One of the issues related to stress was work/life balance. While everyone was having fun drinking beer, once the novelty wore off, what most of them wanted was to get home to their family or off to the gym on their way home from work. We've learned a lot through experimentation, but we have to keep listening to the employees and stay in conversation with them," added Nancy.

"Sometimes we need to try things before we know the right answer. I'm glad the bowling is working out. It is much more in alignment with the values and culture of the organization," suggested Bob.

"Exactly. So we moved to bowling as the social activity, done on company time, during the workday. Everyone is much happier with this solution. And you are right about trying things. It showed everyone that it is okay to try something and acknowledge that it may not work right the first time. It was a great lesson for all of us," admitted Nancy. "And these are just a few examples. Putting our focus on employee well-being is paying off in so many ways."

"Well, that sounds like much of what you are doing is having very positive impact. Hearing the energy in your voice, it sure sounds like you've created a thriving hive," joked Bob.

"I think you are right. And turning things around happened so much faster with your help and learning all that I did when you introduced me to the bees and the thriving hive," acknowledged Nancy. "Bob, it's clear when we put the needs of the employees ahead of every other need in the business, that it changes everything for the better."

Reflection Questions

Take a few minutes to reflect on the lessons Nancy learned from the Dive Hive and the Alive Hive. Use these questions as a guide in your reflection.

Your Organization
- What changes could you make to become a more people-centric workplace?
- What are the benefits to your organization to becoming more people-centric?
- How will your stakeholders (customers, community, investors) benefit from becoming more people-centric?
- What policies in the workplace can be enhanced to support employee well-being?

Managing Oneself
- How can you personally benefit by practicing more self-care?
- What one habit can you adopt that will impact your life and the lives of those around you in a positive way?

Acknowledgments

As an author, I've been blessed to have a tremendous team of people to support me on this journey. I am deeply grateful for your support and encouragement. While I can't possibly list everyone that influenced me on this ride, I do want to thank a few people who have been especially helpful with the creation of this book.

My clients have given me the opportunity to observe, assess, and learn from the workplaces you have created. You have also given me the opportunity to influence both the culture of the workplace and the well-being of your employees.

I am grateful for the CEOs who were willing to be interviewed for this book. Thanks to: Mike Motta, Vin DeProssino, Kip Hollister, Stan Erck, Scott Silk, Dan Moscatiello, Linda Moulton, Mike Standing, Terry Gardiner, and Todd Defren. Special thanks to Susan Stoltze for her work on transcribing the interviews.

This book would not have come to life without the careful and patient guidance of my book coach and editor Claudia Gere. We both ventured into new territory with the parable format. The results are even better than I could have imagined.

The look and feel of a book are greatly dependent on the graphics of the cover and in this case the illustrations in the book. Thanks to Julie Tallman for graphic design support and Rampel (Iwilldovector) for the illustrations.

You never know how a book is going to be received until someone else reads it. Special thanks to Stephen Carr and Nancy Yahanda for being early reviewers and for your invaluable honesty and feedback.

Special thanks to fellow authors, who shared their knowledge and experience. Laura Putnam, Louis Gudema, and Steve Lishansky. Special shout-out to my book launch coach Robbie Samuels, for the step-by-step guidance on creating a successful launch.

Thanks to my launch team. You've been tremendously helpful with suggestions for the subtitle, reading ahead of launch, reviews and social media postings.

I knew very little about bees when I started this book. But having never been a beekeeper, I needed help from those who have hands-on experience. Special thanks to Itzi Garcia, beekeeper extraordinaire.

And finally thanks to my family and friends who supported and encouraged me on this journey, and in so many of my other adventures. Couldn't have done it without you.

Recommended Reading

I have read many books that helped shape my thinking about people-centric workplaces. Here are a few for your continued reading.

Chapman, B., and R. Sisodia. *Everybody Matters: The Extraordinary Power of Caring for Your People Like Family.* New York: Portfolio, 2015.

Chouinard, Y. *Let My People Go Surfing: The Education of a Reluctant Businessman.* New York: Penguin, 2005.

Hougaard, R., and J. Carter. *The Mind of the Leader: How to Lead Yourself, Your People, and Your Organization for Extraordinary Results.* Boston: Harvard Business Review Press, 2018.

Hsieh, T. *Delivering Happiness: A Path to Profits, Passion, and Purpose.* New York: Grand Central Publishing, 2010.

Lencioni, P. *The Advantage: Why Organizational Health Trumps Everything Else in Business.* San Francisco: Jossey-Bass, 2012.

Mackey, J., and R. Sisodia. *Conscious Capitalism: Liberating the Heroic Spirit of Business.* Boston: Harvard Business Review Press, 2014.

Putnam, L. *Workplace Wellness That Works: 10 Steps to Infuse Well-Being and Vitality into Any Organization.* Hoboken: Wiley, 2015.

Rhoades, A. *Built on Values: Creating an Enviable Culture that Outperforms the Competition.* San Francisco: Jossey-Bass, 2011.

Sinek, S. *Leaders Eat Last: Why Some Teams Pull Together and Others Don't.* New York: Portfolio, 2014.

Sisodia, R., J. Sheth, and D. Wolfe. *Firms of Endearment: How World-Class Companies Profit from Passion and Purpose.* Upper Saddle River: Pearson Education, 2014.

On Bees

For the purposes of this story, I've taken some liberties in writing about how a bee colony is organized and functions. So as to avoid attack by thousands of beekeepers and entomologists, this section clarifies how hives actually function. It may also serve to clarify some myths and misconceptions about honeybees.

Honeybees are one of the over 20,000 species of bees in the world today and are the best-known insect on the planet. They are descendants of vegetarian wasps that lived over 100 million years ago. In North America, managed honeybees pollinate over 50 fruits and vegetables that make up a nutritious diet.

A honeybee colony is a complex, democratically organized system, with as many as 50,000 bees in a hive. A typical daily death rate in a hive is 500 bees. The bees perform many different functions in the hive, including:

- Scouting and foraging for pollen, nectar, and water
- Feeding the larvae

- Cleaning the nest
- Processing pollen and nectar into honey
- Building honeycomb by secreting wax from their abdomen
- Protecting the nest from attack by robbers and predators

A honeybee colony is made up of the worker bees (daughters of a single queen bee) and drones (sons of the queen). Honeybees have six legs, five eyes, and four wings. A typical honeybee, born during the spring or summer, will live for six to seven weeks. Bees can fly at 9 to 15 miles per hour, with a trip lasting 5 to 15 minutes. In a single foraging trip, a bee can visit as few as 75 flowers and up to 3,000. All of the foraging bees combined from one hive can visit as many as 225,000 flowers in a single day. It takes about 556 foraging bees to visit 2 million flowers to make a pound of honey. Bees sleep between five and eight hours a day, just like humans.

Unlike the queen bees represented in *The Thriving Hive*, the queen is not in charge and there is no management team. A hive has only one queen at a time and very few bees interact with the queen. The queen's role is to mate with drones, to lay eggs, and to begin new colonies by swarming. The queen can lay as many as 1,000 eggs per day. Queens can live as long as two to three years.

The role of drone (male) bees is to mate with the queen. Unlike other worker bees, drones don't have stingers and don't forage for pollen and nectar. Drone bees help with ventilation of the hive by moving their wings to exhaust air. Upon successful mating with a queen, a drone dies soon thereafter. Drones only mate with virgin queens from another hive, not from their own hive. They are seeking another DNA pool.

The hive is made up of hexagonal cells called honeycombs. The bees construct the honeycombs from wax excreted from their abdomen. Bees eat eight pounds of honey to produce one pound of beeswax.

As a bee visits a flower it collects pollen (protein) and nectar (carbohydrate). The nectar is stored in a body part called the honey sac. They carry the pollen balls in a body part called the pollen basket. Upon returning to the hive, the pollen is mixed with the nectar to form beebread, a protein fed to the larvae. The nectar is combined with enzymes and stored in the honeycomb. By cooling the mixture with their wings, honey is created. Each honeycomb is then capped with beeswax.

Bees need water just like humans and our pets. Bees need a sip of water to keep cool on a hot day.

Water is also important in other hive functions, such as diluting honey to produce food for the larvae, to dissolve crystallized honey, and for cooling the hive during warm weather.

Swarming is the way beehives reproduce. Reasons for swarming include:

- A hive getting overcrowded/congested
- Overheating or poor ventilation
- A declining or failing queen

In a typical swarm, a large quantity of bees flies off with the old queen to a new nest site. The site has been scouted by up to a hundred nest-scout bees. Once a good location is found, the scout bees return to the hive and perform the figure-eight waggle dance to describe the attributes of the site she scouted.

The term hive dive can refer to multiple beekeepers inspecting a hive together, or a significant decline in hive population due to starvation, cold, or pests.

I hope you've had as much fun as I have learning about bees and how important they are. Next time you bite into an apple or munch a handful of nuts, thank the bees.

Resources on Bees

While many of the roles and habits of bees have been inaccurately portrayed in the telling of this story, many books, articles, and other references provided a basis of truth. To find out more about the incredible lives of bees and their colonies, here are many of the references used in writing this book.

Bee-and-Bee-Keeping.com. "The Worker Bee Does It All." http://www.bees-and-beekeeping.com/worker-bee.html

Beemaniacs.com. "Cells, cells, cells," April 18, 2015. https://beemaniacs.com/2015/04/18/cells-cells-and-cells/

Bonoan, R. E. and R. R. Goldman, P. Y. Wong, P. T. Starks. *TuftsNow*, "How Honey Bees Stay Cool," July 23, 2014. http://now.tufts.edu/news-releases/how-honey-bees-stay-cool.

Burlew, Rusty. "Beekeeping: a hobby brimming with possibility," July 7, 2016.
https://honeybeesuite.com/beekeeping-a-hobby-brimming-with-possibility/

Burlew, Rusty. "Do Honeybees Sleep? Of Course They Sleep!" September 1, 2010.
https://honeybeesuite.com/do-honey-bees-sleep-of-course-they-sleep/

Burlew, Rusty. "When Will a Newly-Emerged Queen Begin to Lay?" April 19,2016.
https://honeybeesuite.com/when-will-newly-hatched-queen-begin-lay/

Burlew, Rusty. "You Be the Judge," January 8, 2015.
https://honeybeesuite.com/you-be-the-judge/

Burns, David. "Lesson Twelve: The Moisture Level of Honey," October 28, 2007.
http://basicbeekeeping.blogspot.com/2007/10/lesson-twelve-moisture-level-of-honey.html

Collison, Clarence. *Bee Culture*, "The Queen's Court," March 16, 2017.
http://www.beeculture.com/a-closer-look-8/

Hiskey, Daven. "How Do Bees Produce a Queen Bee," May 17, 2012.

http://www.todayifoundout.com/index.php/2012/05/how-do-bees-produce-a-queen-bee/

Perkins, Sid. "Bees Buzz Each Other, but Not the Way You Think," March 27, 2013 http://www.sciencemag.org/news/2013/03/bees-buzz-each-other-not-way-you-think

Phang. "City Bees Blogspot: Packing in the Pollen," March 13, 2006. http://citybees.blogspot.com/2006/03/packing-in-pollen_13.html.

Sammataro, D. and A. Avitabile. *The Beekeeper's Handbook.* Ithica: Cornell University Press, 2011.

Seedles. "Why Honeybees Need Water," July 7, 2015. https://growtherainbow.com/blogs/news/357301 15-why-honey-bees-need-water

Seeley, Thomas. *Honeybee Democracy.* Princeton: Princeton University Press, 2010.

Southern Oregon Beekeepers Association. "Can It Get Too Hot for Bees?" July 14, 2015. http://www.southernoregonbeekeepers.org/faqs/can-it-get-too-hot-for-bees

Spector, Dina. June 22, 2013. "What Our World Would Look Like Without Honeybees," http://www.businessinsider.com/the-world-without-honeybees-2013-6.

Winston, Mark L. *Bee Time: Lessons from the Hive.* Cambridge: Harvard University Press, 2014.

Create a Thriving Hive in Your Organization

Book Bulk Purchases

To request information about discounted bulk sales email: info@pequossettepress.com.

Speaking and Consulting

Mari Ryan delivers her models for improving employee well-being, workplace culture, and employee engagement to thousands of leaders each year. Whether you're rolling out a new culture initiative, developing a strategy for employee well-being, developing your leaders, or seeking a thought-provoking, engaging and relevant keynote address for your group, Mari and her team can help.

Photo Credit: Kimberly Jones ©2015

To see videos of Mari speaking, visit:
www.youtube.com/c/AdvancingWellnessLLC.

Email info@advwellness.com to schedule Mari to speak at your event or work with your team on a workplace well-being strategy.

About the Author

As CEO and founder of Advancing Wellness, Mari is a workplace well-being strategist guiding organizations to create people-centric workplaces. Working with businesses of all sizes from start-ups to global powerhouses such as Microsoft, Morgan Stanley, and Northrup Grumman, she brings a wealth of experience and expertise.

Mari holds a BA from Lesley University, an MBA from Boston University, and an MS in Health Promotion from Nebraska Methodist College. Her certifications include: Worksite Wellness Program Consultant, Wellness Practitioner, and facilitator in a number of evidence-based behavior change programs. Mari is also a master trainer for the Work@Health program for the Centers for Disease Control and Prevention (CDC).

Mari actively serves or has served on many nonprofit and educational boards including: co-founder of the Worksite Wellness Council of Massachusetts, Board of Directors of Health Promotion Advocates, co-chair of the Smaller Business Association of New England (SBANE) Human Resources Committee, member of the External Advisory Committee for the Center for Promotion of Health in the New England Workplace, a NIOSH-funded Center of Excellence at the University of Massachusetts – Lowell, member of several Human Resource organizations, including the New England Human Resource Association (NEHRA) and Human Resources Leadership Foundation (HRLF).

The *American Journal of Health Promotion, Insights* (NEHRA), and *Occupational Health and Safety Magazine* have published Mari's worksite health promotion articles. Mari is an in-demand speaker at local and national conferences on workplace well-being and talent management topics.

Mari's love for walking brought her to lead a community-based program in Watertown, Massachusetts, called Watertown Walks! As a member of the Watertown Bicycle/Pedestrian committee, Mari initiated a Safe Routes to School program to encourage children to walk or bike to school. In 2006, Mari accomplished a personal goal of climbing Mount Kilimanjaro in Tanzania. In 2016, Mari walked 100 miles of the Camino de Santiago in Spain.